URBAN KNIT COLLECTION

REVISED 2ND EDITION

18 CITY-INSPIRED KNITTING PATTERNS FOR THE MODERN WARDROBE

Kyle Kunnecke

DAVID & CHARLES
—PUBLISHING—

www.davidandcharles.com

TABLE OF CONTENTS

4 INTRODUCTION
A New Home in the City

6 CHAPTER ONE
Planning the Trip: Advice for the City Knitter

16 CHAPTER TWO
Sightseeing: Sweaters for the Journey

- 18 Godfrey Cardigan
- 26 Brandt Pullover
- 32 Arabella Pullover
- 38 Deco Cardigan
- 46 Edwin Vest
- 54 Savoy Cardigan
- 64 Rosema Wrap

70 CHAPTER THREE
A Change in Seasons: Wraps & Scarves

- 72 Apollo Wrap
- 78 D'Amour Wrap
- 90 Arches Scarf
- 94 Sunburst Shawl
- 100 Zephyr Scarf

108 CHAPTER FOUR
Souvenir Shopping: Accessories

- 110 Town-Square Hats
- 116 Ritz Cowl
- 122 Ellington Mittens
- 128 Dorian Cowl
- 132 Skyscraper Hat
- 136 Farmers' Market Mitts

- 140 Glossary
- 141 Techniques
- 155 Bibliography
- 157 Index
- 159 Acknowledgments

INTRODUCTION

A New Home in the City

When *Urban Knit Collection* was first published in 2016, I was living in San Francisco—a city full of color, contrast, and unexpected architectural beauty. Its mix of painted Victorians, quiet bungalows, sharp modern lines, and historic facades became the backdrop for many of the designs in this collection. Surrounded by so much history and beauty, it felt like the right place to bring the book to life. But the inspiration for this work reaches further back—well before I ever picked up a pair of knitting needles.

It began in childhood, during road trips through the hills of southern Indiana and the Midwest. I remember the awe I felt crossing the Ohio River into Louisville, watching the skyline rise in the distance and realizing that every single structure had been built by hand. My dad, a construction superintendent, sometimes took me to work with him. He showed me how to read blueprints and how every project came together bit by bit. He showed me that sometimes things had to be torn back and done over, and explained that it's our goal in life not to be perfect, but to always do the very best we can. That experience left me with a deep appreciation for thoughtful planning, careful execution, and the value of doing things right the first time.

While my dad taught me about managing larger than life projects, it was my mom and grandmothers who introduced me to the magic of the textile arts. I would sit nearby and watch as, stitch by stitch, objects came to life. Their creativity shaped my earliest experiences of craft—and laid the foundation for the work I do now. When the first edition of this book arrived in print, I was lucky enough to share it with my mom. Seeing her hold it—and being able to thank her for her unwavering support—remains one of the greatest joys of my life.

Since the original publication, my own journey has continued. In 2017, I relocated to the Pacific Northwest, where I've become even more immersed in the fiber world—teaching, designing, and working closely with others who are passionate about making.

While the landscape may have changed, my love for the fiber arts (and all things creative!) continues to grow.

This second edition of *Urban Knit Collection* gave me the chance to revisit the original with fresh eyes. While the photography and pattern offerings remain unchanged, I've updated some of the language, corrected technical errors, and made small refinements to improve clarity. It's being published through David & Charles, and I'm grateful for the opportunity to share it again with new readers and longtime supporters alike.

The patterns in this collection remain a love letter to structure, texture, and timeless design. They were created with the understanding that it's okay to give ourselves time for our passions. Like the buildings that inspired them, these pieces are meant to last. They ask for care and attention while being crafted, and in return, they offer a sense of accomplishment and pride knowing the completed works can be enjoyed for generations.

If you're returning to this book, welcome back. And if this is your first time picking it up, I hope you find inspiration, challenge, and beauty in these projects—just as I did when creating them.

Happy knitting,

Kyle

CHAPTER ONE

Planning the Trip: Advice for the City Knitter

Landing in a new city is always exciting. Through research before the journey, we can discover some of the icons that make a place unique and have a list of things we want to experience during our stay.

When visiting San Francisco, California, for example, the Golden Gate Bridge, Chinatown, or Alcatraz may come to mind. Every city has a few landmarks that help us find our way, such as the town square, the old church, the mansion on the hill, and experiences such as eating at a certain restaurant, staying at a well-loved bed and breakfast, discovering exhibits at the museum, or shopping at the local yarn boutiques. Being prepared before the journey helps us get around and feel more comfortable as we explore.

Similarly, keeping these tips in mind should be useful throughout your knitting journey.

Hollywood, California: Home sick one day from work, I sat on the couch watching daytime television with my roommate, Debra. I was wrapped up in a blanket, eating a bowl of cereal, watching her knit row after row on a multi-striped garter-stitch scarf. The process looked complicated and boring to me. I questioned her desire to do such a tedious craft.

Knowing I like making things, she challenged me to give knitting a try. She cast on and taught me the first stitch. I knit, knit, knit for hours, concentrating and studying how the yarn forms loops and links together, mesmerized by the idea that knitted fabric is made up of one long piece of yarn. It was amazing—and it was frustrating. My first project was full of holes and knots, its width grew and shrank, and although I was proud (because I was learning), I knew that I could do better.

This was only my first afternoon of knitting and already I was obsessed. Off we went to the local yarn shop where I bought my first skein of yarn and my very own set of needles. I cast on for my first scarf, knowing to take my time, work one row, and then count the stitches. From there, I spent a few years (yes, years!) knitting garter-stitch striped scarves and blankets.

After moving from Hollywood to the outskirts of Los Angeles, I started hanging out at my new local yarn shop. It was there that one of the customers helped guide me toward knitting patterns. At first patterns seemed intimidating, but once I understood the skills required for each design, I realized that knitting is not difficult; it just takes time.

TIME VS DIFFICULTY

Looking at a project can be overwhelming. Imagine building a house. Or a skyscraper. Or an entire city! How was the Internet built? How did we put a man on the moon? I look at the city skyline at night with all its lights and become mesmerized at the thought of how much time and work it took to install all those light bulbs. How do large projects get done? We get things done, my friend John says, "The same way you eat an elephant: One bite at a time."

It's okay to be overwhelmed at the detail involved in a project. It's okay to walk away from complicated projects if you don't have the time or space to concentrate on them—but don't dismiss them because you think they are difficult. They aren't.

Knitted fabric is essentially made of two stitches: knit and purl. And if we get really technical about it, those two stitches are the same, just turned around. The other steps needed build on the basics. Give yourself the time to experiment and practice, and you'll be prepared to knit anything you want!

A WORD ABOUT SKILL LEVEL

Knitting patterns break down a project into a series of steps. If you follow those steps, generally you end up with a nicely finished project.

When we take away the labels that are sometimes attached to patterns, reserving each specifically for beginning, intermediate, or advanced knitters, we may realize that the instructions speak for themselves—and directly to the knitter. If you have the skills that are specified for a particular project, then you're ready to cast on. If you don't, then you know what skills you need to learn before you begin.

In this book, I outlined the various skills that you need for knitting each project in a list called "Knitting Knowledge." It's not that the patterns are easy or difficult. It's really about knowing how to perform the steps involved. We mislabel tasks as being difficult when really we mean that they're time-consuming. While some take longer than others, I'm confident you can make any project in this book.

BLEEDING YARNS

We all want our projects to be beautifully finished. If you are at all concerned about the color from one yarn bleeding to another when wet, use your gauge swatch to put your worries to rest. Soak it in cool water as normal and look for signs that the dye from the yarn is leaking into the water. If the water remains clear, the dye in the yarn is most likely set.

If the water is not clear, then wind the yarn into a hank using a yarn swift or the back of a chair, and tie the end and beginning together. Secure the hank in a few places with pieces of string using a figure eight: Divide the hank in half, wrap one half with the string, cross the strings over each other, and then wrap them around the second half of the hank. Tie the two ends together. Soak the yarn in a cool bath of water with a generous splash of white vinegar. Drain, rinse, and repeat with cool water to ensure the water remains clear.

Lift the hank out of the water; press the water out of the yarn by folding it into a towel, then hang it on plastic hangers to dry. Do not hang a weight on the bottom of the hank as this will stretch the yarn.

Yes, all of this—re-winding the yarn, soaking it, and letting it hang dry for hours (or even days)—takes more time. It cuts at that ingrained desire to cast on immediately. I guarantee, though, that once you've done this, it'll eliminate any fear you had about too much dye in the yarn ruining your project.

TASTE TESTING

Why is it that so many knitters don't take time to swatch? Swatches are like knitting warm-ups or like being able to taste lots of different flavors of ice cream before committing to an entire bowl. It's a chance to experiment with ideas you might have about altering a pattern, such as changing the type of ribbing or experimenting with a color combination or a certain motif. They provide time to become familiar with new stitch patterns, allow us to check out what type of fabric the yarn will become, and provide us with valuable information regarding row and stitch gauge. The neat thing about swatching? Every time you knit something that needs to measure a certain dimension, you're doing it!

I tell my students that you must swatch. There's no way around it. The choice you make is this: Do you want to swatch a small bit of fabric so that you are able to confirm gauge, drape, etc., or do you begin by diving into a project headfirst, casting on hundreds of stitches, working on the project for hours (or days) before coming to the realization that the gauge is off or that the fabric isn't looking the way you had hoped? All that work, only to rip it all out, change needle size, and cast on again. Either way, you're swatching.

Sometimes, gauge is important, such as when making a sweater. Other times, the drape of the finished fabric is more important than achieving a certain size, such as when making a wrap or scarf. While working up your swatches for the projects in this book, be sure you're knitting them in the manner indicated in the instructions.

See page 152 to learn about speed swatching in the round.

RIPPING OUT

I've never met someone who regretted fixing a mistake.

First, it's okay to make mistakes when crafting. Looking back at the progress of a project, it is inevitable that sooner or later you'll find a cable that's crossed wrong or a stitch pattern that's slightly askew. While it can be frustrating (and sometimes downright depressing) to come to the decision to rip out hours and hours of work, the pride you'll feel after correcting a mistake is worth it. Take your time, study your knitting, and don't be afraid to rip. After all, reknitting is knitting . . . and we love to knit, don't we?

True confession time: While I was knitting the sample Savoy Cardigan (page 54) for this book, I ignored my own advice and pressed on through the back, both sleeves, and one entire side of the garment before accepting the reality that I needed to make a small shaping change in the pattern. It was a small change that needed to happen, but there wasn't a way to fix it while being true to the instructions. This (of course) sent me into a bout of denial.

The back was complete, and I knew what had to be done. But I pressed on, hoping (I guess) that some sort of miracle would happen and suddenly things would work out. Here's the reality: Mistakes don't fix themselves. Sometimes, we can find ways to work around them, but more often than not, the mistake lives on unless we do something to address it. The day came when I had no choice but to face the task of ripping back so that I could have the best finished project possible to include in the book. So don't feel bad if you discover that the only way to move forward is to rip back.

LOCKING FLOATS

Traditional Fair Isle—or stranded knitting—typically uses no more than two colors per row or round, with colors changed or floats trapped every inch or less. The yarn held in the left hand or lower position appears more prominent (the dominant color) because its slightly longer floats allow the stitches to relax. Keeping the yarns in the same order throughout the project ensures consistent color dominance.

There are several ways to hold two yarns: one in each hand, or both in the same hand. Regardless of method, the yarn in the the left-most yarn (or below) will appear more prominently in the fabric. This is your dominant color.

Stranded knitting creates floats across the back that can snag. One solution is to trap the unused yarn behind the work. While often called Armenian knitting, similar techniques appear in many cultural traditions. I use the term locked floats to describe the method without attributing it to a single origin. This method has been around for nearly a century—Elsa Schiaparelli's 1927 Bowknot Sweater is a well-known example.

To lock floats, follow a simple rhythm: work the first stitch of a new color normally, then trap the unused yarn behind every other subsequent stitch. Reset this rhythm each time you change colors. Locking floats consistently builds muscle memory—your knitting will flow more smoothly, and you won't need to pause to check where to trap the yarn. The stitch immediately following the lock completes the process and secures the trapped yarn in place. This approach creates a dense, balanced fabric with a woven-like reverse and helps resolve common tension issues. You *can* lock floats less frequently, but the less often you do, the more the effect of color dominance begins to return.

Springy yarns tend to reduce the chance of seeing the locked color from the front, though it may occasionally peek through. This isn't a flaw—it's part of the fabric's story. Swatching will help you see how your yarn behaves. If needed, these peeking floats can often be nudged to the back with the tip of a needle.

You'll find step-by-step photo tutorials on the following pages. Scan the QR code or visit **kylewilliam.com/techniques** for video guidance.

Planning the Trip

Locking Floats - Two-Handed

Hold the dominant color in your left hand and the second color in your right. This places the dominant yarn in the lower position on the back of the work. After locking a float, the yarns are wrapped around each other. The next stitch of the same color uses this twist to complete the stitch.

Knit Stitch | Two-Handed | Locking Left Yarn

1. Insert needle knit-wise into stitch. Move working needle under LY, maintaining tension on yarn.

2. Wrap RY around needle knit-wise.

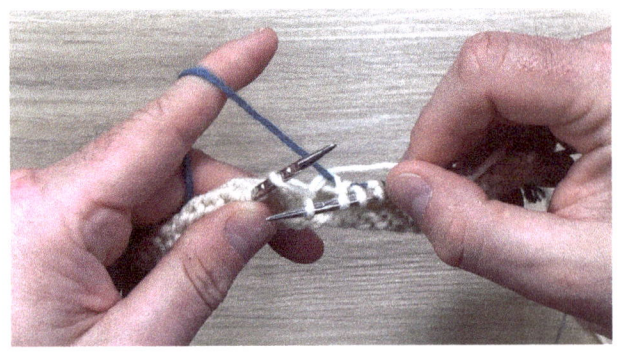

3. Return LY to back of work. Complete stitch.

Knit Stitch | Two-Handed | Locking Right Yarn

1. Insert needle knit-wise into stitch. Wrap RY around needle.

2. Follow in the same direction with LY.

3. Unwrap RY from needle to back of work. Complete stitch.

Purl Stitch | Two-Handed | Locking Left Yarn

1. Insert needle purl-wise into stitch. Move LY between needles, maintaining tension.

2. Wrap RY around needle as if to purl (counter-clockwise).

3. Bring RY back down below work. Complete stitch.

Purl Stitch | Two-Handed | Locking Right Yarn

1. Insert needle purl-wise into stitch. Wrap RY clockwise (opposite way from purling).

2. Wrap LY around needle as if to purl (counter-clockwise).

3. Keeping LY in place, unwrap RY. Complete stitch.

Locking Floats - Continental

Hold the dominant color to the left (closer to your palm) and the second color to the right. This keeps the dominant yarn in the lower position on the back of the work. After locking a float, the yarns are twisted. The next stitch of the same color is worked above this twist to finish locking the float.

Knit Stitch | Continental Locking Left-Most Yarn

1. Insert needle knit-wise into stitch and between yarns.

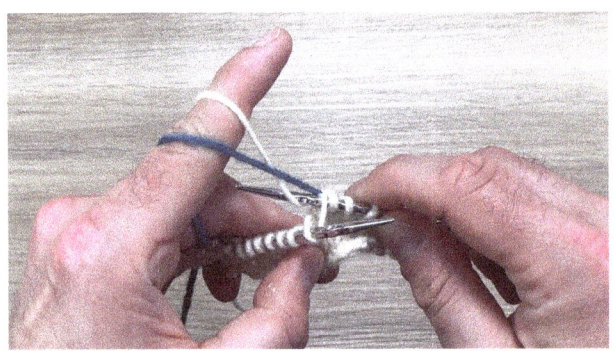

2. Move needle clockwise over RY and back under LY.

3. Complete stitch with RY.

Knit Stitch | Continental Locking Right-Most Yarn

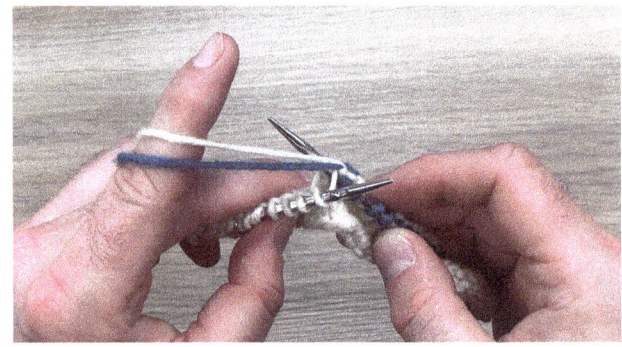

1. Insert needle purl-wise into stitch and under both yarns.

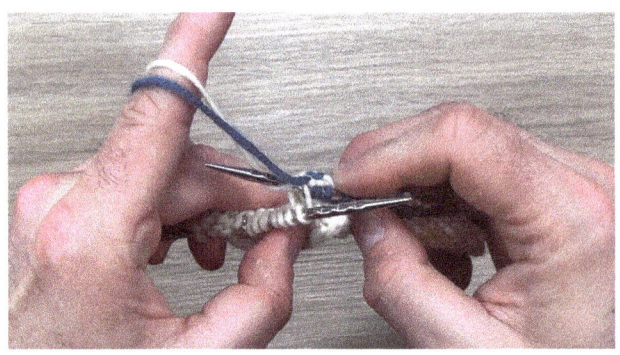

2. Move needle over RY and under LY.

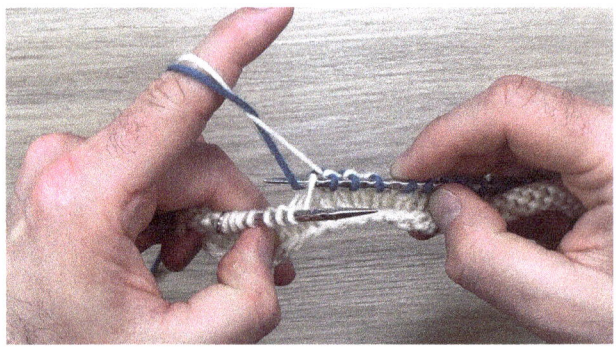

3. Reversing direction, return needle back under both yarns, trapping RY. Complete stitch.

Purl Stitch | Continental
Locking Left-Most Yarn

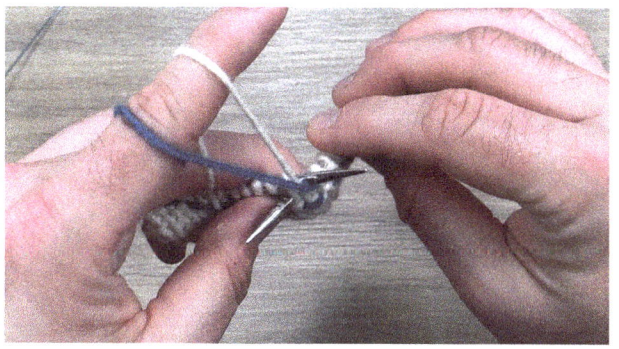

1. Insert working needle purl-wise into stitch under both yarns.

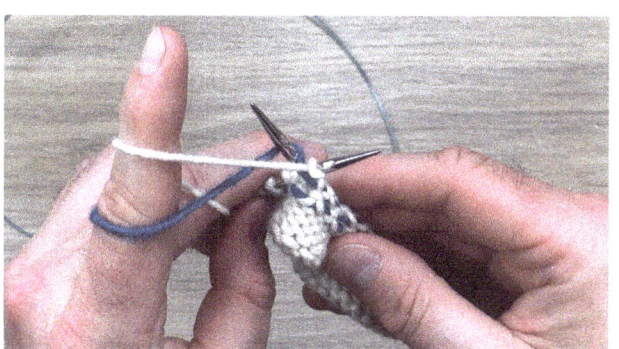

2. Bring working needle over LY and under RY.

3. Reversing direction, move tip of needle counter-clockwise back under LY. (RY now on needle.) Complete stitch.

Purl Stitch | Continental
Locking Right-Most Yarn

1. Insert working needle purl-wise into stitch and under both yarns.

2. Swing needle up over RY and under LY.

3. Move tip of working needle clockwise back over RY (LY now on needle) and complete stitch.

See Techniques pages 153-154 for information on shaping and short-rows in colorwork knitting.

CHAPTER TWO

Sightseeing: Sweaters for the Journey

Heading out to explore the city, it's exciting to imagine what the day might bring. In the unpredictable weather of San Francisco, carrying a warm layer or two is a must in case the fog rolls in or the temperature takes a dip.

If I'm out and about, I usually carry a bag packed with essentials, including a knitting project. Believe it or not, sweaters are among my favorite portable projects. Worked in pieces, they require enough technique to keep my focus.

Sleeves are usually the first on the needles; it's a chance to study stitch patterns and make sure that my gauge is correct. As a way to ensure that the sleeves are identical in size, I copy or write out the pattern row by row (indicating increase or decrease rows, etc.) on a sheet of paper. I mark through each line as a row is completed. When it's time to create the second sleeve, I use the same pattern notes and highlight or mark each row off the same way. After the sleeves are done, I make the back and then the front (or fronts) before joining and seaming them together into a fantastic, finished piece.

For me, much of the joy in knitting comes not only from the making, but also in the opportunity to connect with others who share a passion for craft. Take these patterns out on the road with you; to cafes, on plane flights, and to knitting groups. The classically styled garments in this book promise to keep you company long after the knitting is completed.

GODFREY CARDIGAN

Inspired by stacked brickwork on an old building in New York City, this saddle-shoulder cardigan is a classic design that boasts an angled textured pattern. Paring the design down to its basic form and using exquisite materials, Godfrey is the kind of cardigan that will stay in style as long as its color lasts. Keeping the first and last few stitches in stockinette while working the individual pieces creates a beautiful finish at the sides and under the arms.

Finished Size
31½ (35½, 39¾, 43½, 48, 51¾)" (80 [90, 101, 110.5, 122, 131.5] cm) bust circumference and 22½ (23¾, 25½, 27, 27½, 27¾)" (57 [60.5, 65, 68.5, 70, 70.5] cm) long.

Cardigan shown measures 35½" (90 cm) with 2" (5 cm) of ease.

Yarn
DK weight (#3 Light).

Shown: Madelinetosh Tosh DK (100% superwash merino; 225 yd [206 m]/100 g): Jade, 5 (6, 7, 7, 8, 9) hanks.

Needles
Size U.S. 5 (3.75 mm): 24" (60 cm) circular (cir) or straight.

Size U.S. 5 (3.75 mm): 40" (100 cm) or longer cir for buttonband.

Size U.S. 6 (4 mm): 24" (60 cm) cir or straight.

Adjust needle sizes if necessary to obtain the correct gauge.

Notions
Stitch markers (m); stitch holders; tapestry needle.

Six ⅞" (22 mm) buttons.

Gauge
21 sts and 30 rows = 4" (10 cm) over patt with larger needles, blocked.

Knitting Knowledge
This project is worked flat and requires:
- Knitting with circular needles
- Casting on and binding off
- Reading charts
- Knitting and purling
- Increasing and decreasing
- Finishing

Notes
Work all of the decreases for the neck shaping inside the neck edge, keeping the last 2 stitches in stockinette stitch. This helps create a clean transition from the body to the buttonband.

Read right-side rows of the chart from right to left and wrong-side rows from left to right.

BACK

Cast on
With smaller needles, CO 84 (94, 106, 116, 128, 138) sts using the German twisted method (Techniques, page 141).

ROW 1: (RS) *K2, p2; rep from * to last 0 (2, 2, 0, 0, 2) sts, k0 (2, 2, 0, 0, 2).

ROW 2: (WS) P0 (2, 2, 0, 0, 2), *k2, p2; rep from * to end.

Cont in established patt until piece measures 2½" (6.5 cm) from CO, ending with a RS row. Change to larger needles.

NEXT ROW: (WS) Purl.

Begin Chart A
NEXT ROW: (RS) K2, place marker (pm), beg at arrow for your size on Chart A, reading Row 1 from right to left, work next 12 (3, 9, 0, 6, 11) sts to left side of chart, beg at right side of chart and work 28-st rep 2 (3, 3, 4, 4, 4) times, work first 12 (3, 9, 0, 6, 11) sts of chart once more, pm, k2.

NEXT ROW: (WS) P2, sm, beg at arrow for your size on right side of Chart A, reading Row 2 from left to right, work 12 (3, 9, 0, 6, 11) sts to right side of chart, beg at left side of chart and work 28-st rep 2 (3, 3, 4, 4, 4) times, work last 12 (3, 9, 0, 6, 11) sts of chart once more, sm, p2.

Work Rows 3–18 as established, then rep Rows 1–18 until piece measures 4" (10 cm) from CO, ending with a WS row.

Shape waist
DEC ROW: (RS) K2, ssk (or ssp to maintain patt), work to last 4 sts, k2tog (or p2tog to maintain patt), k2—2 sts dec'd.

Rep dec row every other RS row 5 (5, 7, 7, 9, 9) more times—72 (82, 90, 100, 108, 118) sts rem.

Work 8 rows even.

INC ROW: (RS) K2, m1 (or m1p to maintain patt), work to last 2 sts, m1 (or m1p to maintain patt), k2—2 sts inc'd.

Rep inc row every other RS row 5 (5, 7, 7, 9, 9) more times—84 (94, 106, 116, 128, 138) sts.

Cont even until piece measures 16 (16½, 17½, 17½, 17½, 17½)" (40.5 [42, 44.5, 44.5, 44.5, 44.5] cm), ending with a WS row.

Shape armholes
BO 5 (6, 7, 8, 9, 10) sts at beg of next 2 rows, 3 (3, 3, 4, 4, 5) sts at beg of next 2 rows, then 2 sts at beg of next 0 (2, 2, 2, 4, 4) rows—68 (72, 82, 88, 94, 100) sts rem.

Dec 1 st at each end every RS row 0 (0, 1, 1, 1, 2) time(s)—68 (72, 80, 86, 92, 96) sts rem.

Cont even until piece measures 20½ (21¾, 23½, 24¾, 25¼, 25¼)" (52 [55, 59.5, 63, 64, 64] cm) from CO.

BO 23 (24, 27, 29, 31, 32) sts at beg of next 2 rows—22 (24, 26, 28, 30, 32) sts rem.

Cont even for 2½ (2¾, 3, 3¼, 3¼, 3½)" (6.5 [7, 7.5, 8.5, 8.5, 9] cm).

Place sts on holder. Cut yarn, leaving a 6" (15 cm) tail.

LEFT FRONT

With smaller needles, CO 38 (42, 46, 54, 58, 62) sts using the German twisted method.

ROW 1: (RS) *K2, p2; rep from * to last 2 sts, k2.

ROW 2: (WS) *P2, k2; rep from * to last 2 sts, p2.

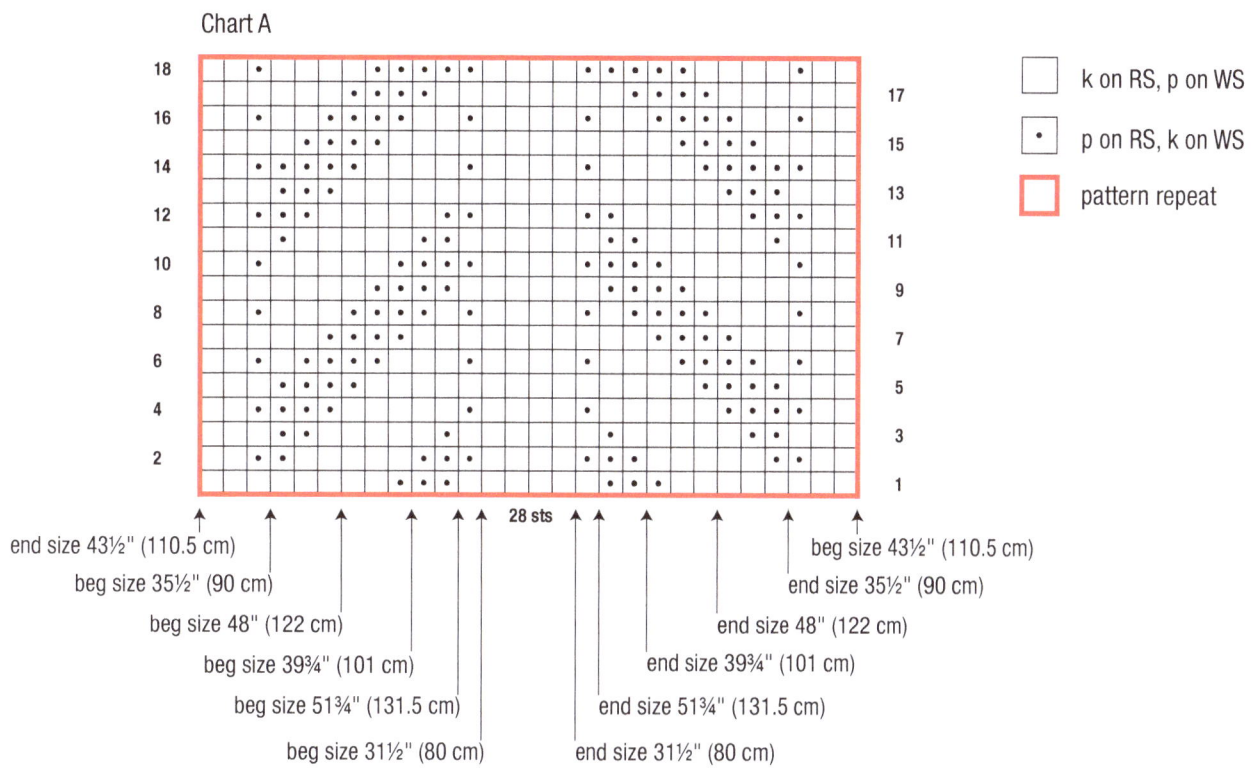

Cont in established patt until piece measures 2½" (6.5 cm) from CO, ending with a WS row.

INC ROW: (RS) Work in established rib and inc 0 (1, 3, 0, 1, 2) st(s) evenly spaced in pattern—38 (43, 49, 54, 59, 64) sts.

Switch to larger needles.

NEXT ROW: (WS): Purl.

Begin Chart B

NEXT ROW: (RS) K2, pm, beg at arrow for your size on Chart B (page 22), reading Row 1 from right to left, work next 8 (13, 19, 24, 1, 6) st(s) to left side of chart, beg at right side of chart and work 28-st rep 0 (0, 0, 0, 1, 1) time(s), work first 26 sts of chart once more, pm, k2.

NEXT ROW: (WS) P2, sm, beg at arrow on Chart B, reading Row 2 from left to right, work next 26 sts to right side of chart, beg at left side of chart and work 28-st rep 0 (0, 0, 0, 1, 1) time(s), then beg at left side of chart and work 8 (13, 19, 24, 1, 6) st(s) once more, p2.

Cont in established patt until piece measures 4" (10 cm) from CO, ending with a WS row.

Shape waist

DEC ROW: (RS) K2, k2tog (or p2tog to maintain patt), work to end—1 st dec'd.

Rep dec row every other RS row 5 (5, 7, 7, 9, 9) more times—32 (37, 41, 46, 49, 54) sts rem.

Work 8 rows even.

INC ROW: (RS) K2, m1 (or m1p to maintain patt), work to end—1 st inc'd.

Rep inc row every other RS row 5 (5, 7, 7, 9, 9) more times—38 (43, 49, 54, 59, 64) sts.

Cont even until piece measures 16 (16½, 17½, 17½, 17½, 17½)" (40.5 [42, 44.5, 44.5, 44.5, 44.5] cm), ending with a WS row.

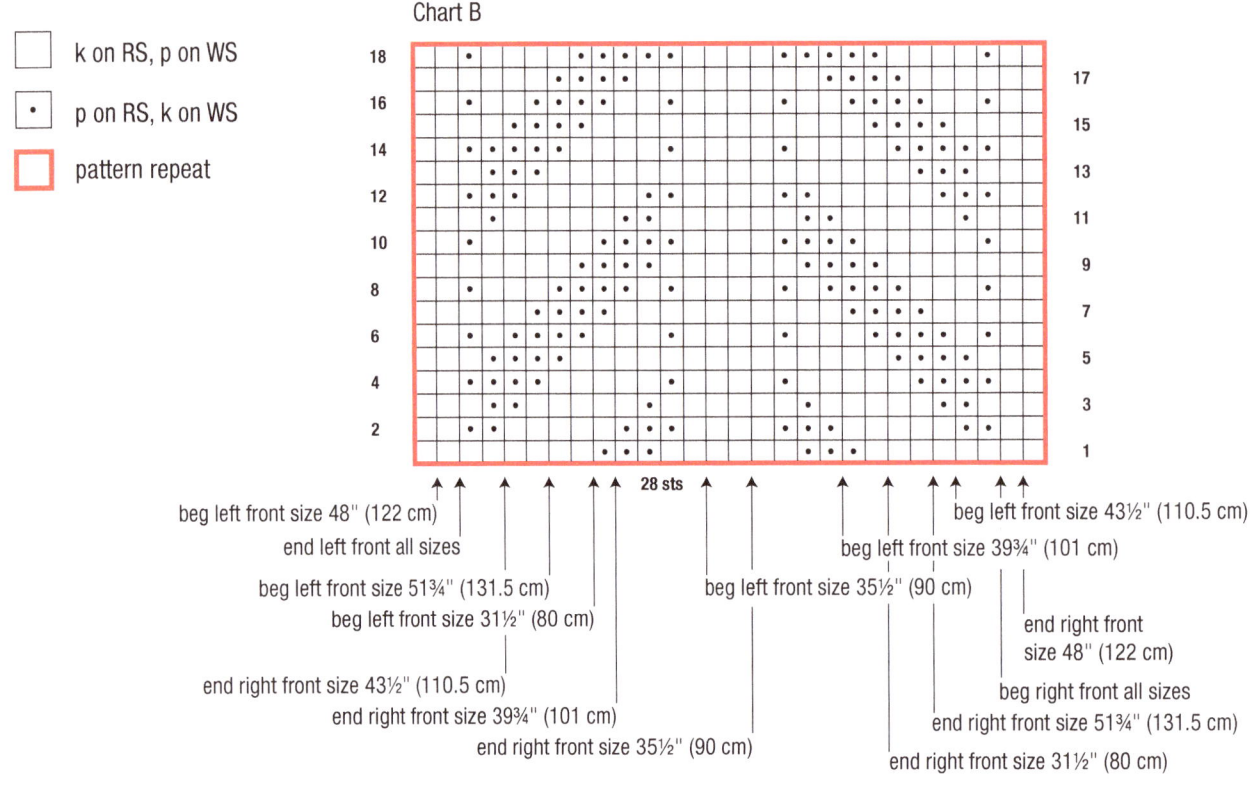

Shape armholes

BO at beg of RS row 5 (6, 7, 8, 9, 10) sts once, 3 (3, 3, 4, 4, 5) sts once, then 2 sts 0 (1, 1, 1, 2, 2) time(s)—30 (32, 37, 40, 42, 45) sts rem.

Dec 1 st at beg of RS row 0 (0, 1, 1, 1, 2) time(s)—30 (32, 36, 39, 41, 43) sts rem.

Shape neck

DEC ROW: (RS) Work to last 4 sts, k2tog (or p2tog to maintain patt), k2—1 st dec'd.

Rep dec row every RS row 7 (9, 11, 11, 13, 13) more times—22 (22, 24, 27, 27, 29) sts rem.

Cont even until piece measures 20½ (21¾, 23½, 24¾, 25¼, 25¼)" (52 [55, 59.5, 63, 64, 64] cm) from CO.

BO rem sts. Cut yarn, leaving a 6" (15 cm) tail.

RIGHT FRONT

With smaller needles, CO 38 (42, 46, 54, 58, 62) sts the using the German twisted method.

ROW 1: (RS) *K2, p2; rep from * to last 2 sts, k2.

ROW 2: (WS) *P2, k2; rep from * to last 2 sts, p2.

Cont in established patt until piece measures 2½" (6.5 cm) from CO, ending with a WS row.

INC ROW: (RS) Work in established rib patt and inc 0 (1, 3, 0, 1, 2) st(s) evenly spaced in patt—38 (43, 49, 54, 59, 64) sts.

Switch to larger needles.

NEXT ROW: (WS) Purl.

Begin Chart B

NEXT ROW: (RS) K2, pm, beg at arrow for all sizes of right front Chart B, reading Row 1 from right to left, work 26 sts to left side of chart, beg at right side of chart and work 28-st rep 0 (0, 0, 0, 1, 1) time(s), beg at right side of chart and work first 8 (13, 19, 24, 1, 6) st(s) once more, pm, k2.

NEXT ROW: (WS) P2, sm, beg at arrow for your size on Row 2 of Chart B, work 8 (13, 19, 24, 1, 6) st(s) to right side of chart, beg at left side of chart and work 28-st rep 0 (0, 0, 0, 1, 1) time(s), beg at left side of chart and work next 26 sts once more, sm, p2.

Cont in established patt until piece measures 4" (10 cm) from CO, ending with a WS row.

Shape waist

DEC ROW: (WS) Work to last 4 sts, k2tog (or p2tog to maintain patt), k2—1 st dec'd.

Rep dec row every other RS row 5 (5, 7, 7, 9, 9) more times—32 (37, 41, 46, 49, 54) sts rem.

Work 8 rows even.

INC ROW: (RS) Work in established patt to last 2 sts, m1 (or m1p to maintain patt), k2—1 st inc'd.

Rep inc row every other RS row 5 (5, 7, 7, 9, 9) more times—38 (43, 49, 54, 59, 64) sts.

Cont even until piece measures 16 (16½, 17½, 17½, 17½, 17½)" (40.5 [42, 44.5, 44.5, 44.5, 44.5] cm), ending with a RS row.

Shape armholes

BO at beg of WS row 5 (6, 7, 8, 9, 10) sts once, 3 (3, 3, 4, 4, 5) sts once, then 2 sts 0 (1, 1, 1, 2, 2) time(s)—30 (32, 37, 40, 42, 45) sts rem.

Dec 1 st at end of RS row 0 (0, 1, 1, 1, 2) time(s)—30 (32, 36, 39, 41, 43) sts rem.

Shape neck

DEC ROW: (RS) K2, k2tog (or p2tog to maintain patt), work to end—1 st dec'd.

Rep dec row every RS row 7 (9, 11, 11, 13, 13) more times—22 (22, 24, 27, 27, 29) sts rem.

Cont even until piece measures 20½ (21¾, 23½, 24¾, 25¼, 25¼)" (52 [55, 59.5, 63, 64, 64] cm) from CO.

BO rem sts. Cut yarn, leaving a 6" (15 cm) tail.

SLEEVES

With smaller needles, CO 38 (42, 46, 46, 50, 54) sts using the German twisted method.

ROW 1: (RS) *K2, p2; rep from * to last 2 sts, k2.

ROW 2: (WS) *P2, k2; rep from * to last 2 sts, p2.

Cont in established patt until piece measures 2" (5 cm) from CO, ending with a WS row.

INC ROW: (RS) Work in established patt and inc 2 (0, 0, 2, 2, 0) sts evenly spaced—40 (42, 46, 48, 52, 54) sts.

Switch to larger needles.

NEXT ROW: (WS) Purl.

Begin Chart C

NEXT ROW: (RS) K2, pm, beg at arrow for your size of Row 1 of Chart C (page 24), work 4 (5, 7, 8, 10, 11) sts to left side of chart, beg at right side of chart and work 28-st rep once, then beg at right side of chart and work first 4 (5, 7, 8, 10, 11) sts once more, pm, k2.

NEXT ROW: (WS) P2, sm, beg at arrow for your size for Row 2 of Chart C, work 4 (5, 7, 8, 10, 11) sts to right side of chart, beg at left side of chart and work 28-st rep once, then beg at left side of chart and work last 4 (5, 7, 8, 10, 11) sts once more, sm, p2.

Cont in established patt, and work 2 more rows even.

INC ROW: (RS) K2, sm, m1 (or m1p to maintain patt), work to last 2 sts, m1 (or m1p to maintain patt), k2—2 sts inc'd.

Rep inc at each end of every 12 (10, 10, 8, 8, 8) rows 4 (10, 6, 10, 8, 4) times, then every 10 (8, 8, 6, 6, 6) rows 5 (1, 6, 5, 9, 15) time(s)—60 (66, 72, 80, 88, 94) sts.

Cont even until piece measures 16½ (17½, 18, 18½, 19, 20)" (42 [44.5, 45.5, 47, 48.5, 51] cm) from CO, ending with a WS row.

Shape sleeve cap

BO 4 (4, 5, 5, 6, 6) sts at beg of next 2 rows, removing markers and discontinuing St st (knit on RS rows, purl on WS rows) edge detail—3 (2, 3, 4, 4, 4) sts at beg of next 2 rows, then 2 sts at beg of next 0 (2, 2, 2, 4, 4) rows—46 (50, 52, 58, 60, 66) sts rem.

Dec 1 st at each end every other RS row 8 (9, 10, 11, 12, 13) times, then every row 4 (5, 5, 6, 6, 7) times—22 (22, 22, 24, 24, 26) sts rem.

Work even until saddle measures 4 (4½, 4¾, 5½, 5½, 6)" (10 [11.5, 12, 14, 14, 15] cm).

Note: To ensure the perfect length of the saddle, place these sts on holder until work is assembled. Add or remove rows until work is the correct length and then BO rem sts. Cut yarn, leaving a 6" (15 cm) tail.

FINISHING

Using mattress stitch (see Techniques), sew side seams and then sleeve saddles to front and back shoulders. Set in sleeves. Sew sleeve seams.

Weave in all ends.

Work buttonband

With smaller long cir needle and RS facing, beg at lower right front, pick up and k116 (123, 134, 141, 144, 145) sts along right front, 14 (14, 14, 16, 16, 18) sts along right saddle, knit held 22 (24, 26, 28, 30, 32) back sts from holder, pick up and k14 (14, 14, 16, 16, 18) sts along left saddle, then 116 (123, 134, 141, 144, 145) sts along left front to bottom edge—282 (298, 322, 342, 350, 358) sts.

Work back and forth.

NEXT ROW: (WS) *P2, k2; rep from * to last 2 sts, p2.

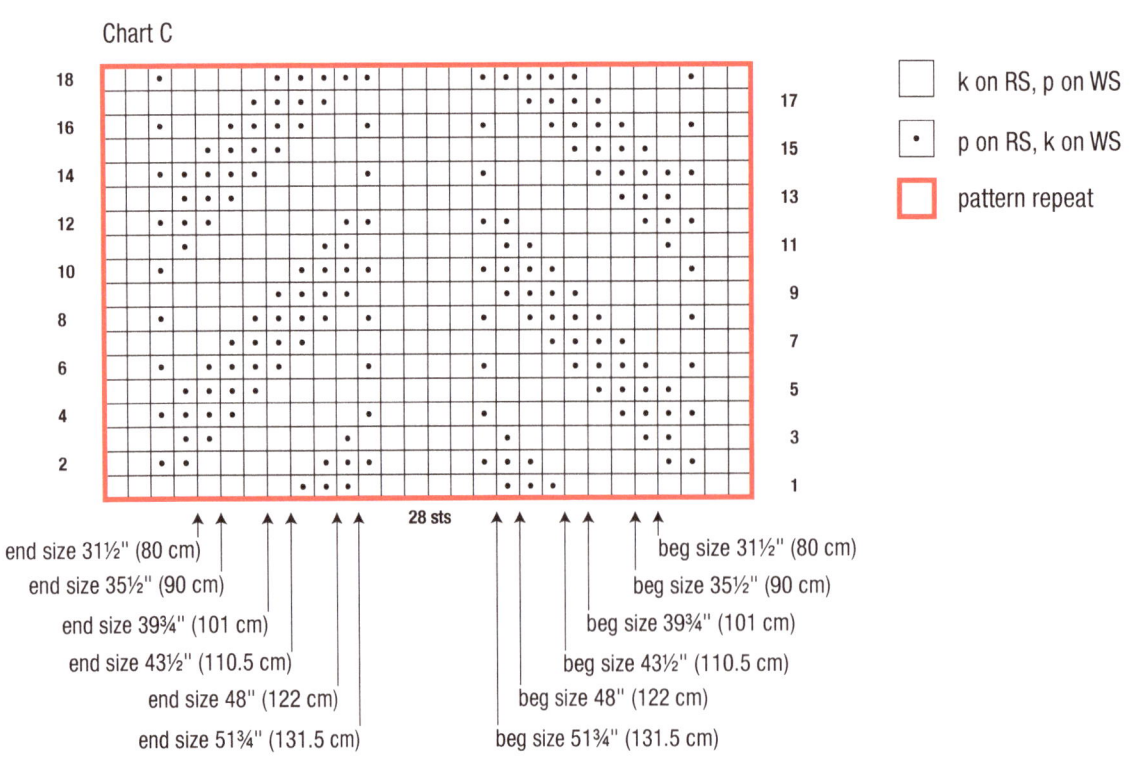

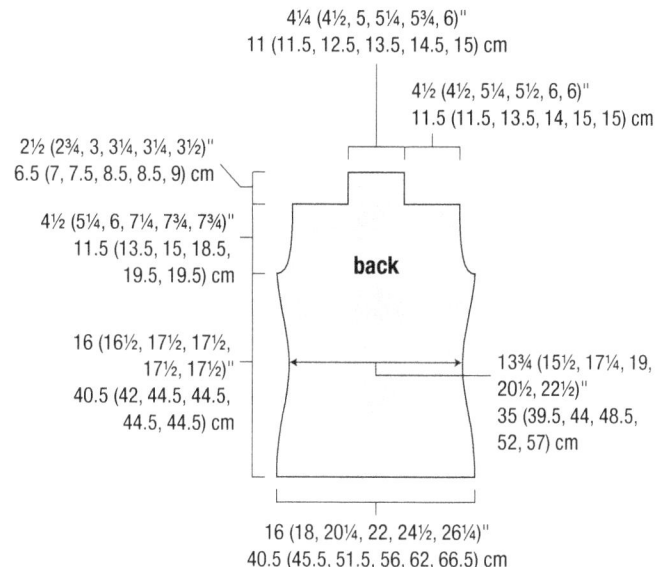
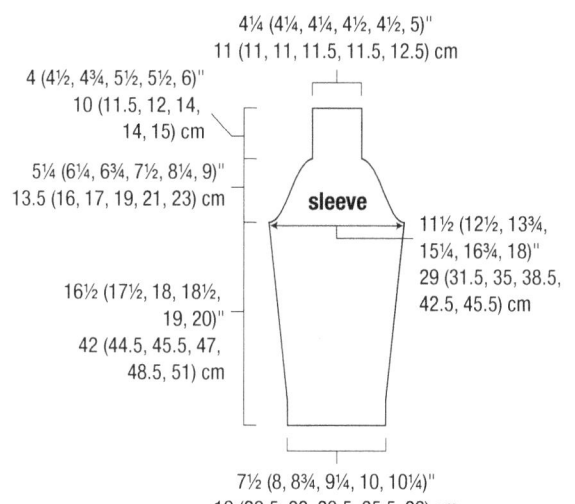
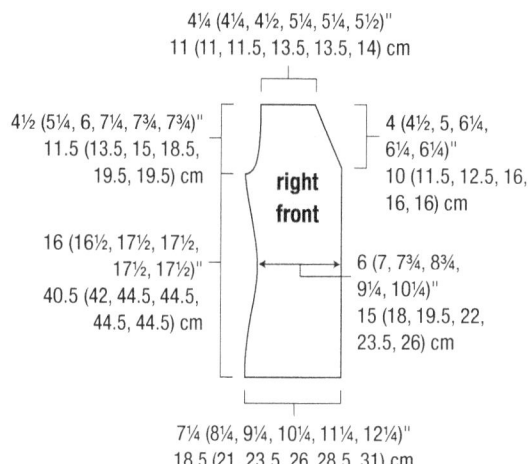

NEXT ROW: (RS) *K2, p2; rep from * to last 2 sts, k2.

Work 1 more row.

Place markers for buttonholes along right front, place top marker at beg of neck shaping, bottom button about ½" (1.3 cm) from bottom edge, then evenly space rem markers in between.

(BUTTONHOLE) ROW: (RS) *Work in established rib patt to 1 st before m, work one-row buttonhole (see Techniques) over next 3 sts; rep from * 5 more times, work in rib to end.

Cont in established rib patt until band measures 1" (2.5 cm). BO all sts in rib. Cut yarn, leaving a 6" (15 cm) tail.

Weave in rem ends, waiting to trim yarn tails until after piece has been blocked.

Soak cardigan in a bath of cool water with a little wool wash. Lift out of bath and gently squeeze to remove water. Lay cardigan on a towel and roll up to remove excess water. Unroll, shape, and lay flat to dry.

Sew buttons to left buttonband opposite buttonholes.

BRANDT PULLOVER

This pullover features a quiet colorwork pattern on the front with a textured stitch filling the arms and back that lies flat, isn't stretchy, and offers texture and a thickness similar to that of the front. For even more impact, consider selecting colors with greater contrast for the front panel.

Finished Size
33¼ (37¼, 41½, 44, 48¼)" (84.5 [94.5, 105.5, 112, 122.5] cm) chest circumference and 24½ (25¼, 27, 27¾, 28)" (62 [64, 68.5, 70.5, 71] cm) long.

Pullover shown measures 44" (112 cm) with 2¼" (5.5 cm) of ease.

Yarn
DK weight (#3 Light).

Shown: Rowan Felted Tweed DK (50% merino, 25% alpaca, 25% viscose; 191 yd [175 m]/50 g): #178 Seasalter (MC), 7 (8, 8, 9, 10) balls; #145 Treacle (CC), 2 (2, 2, 3, 3) balls.

Needles
Size U.S. 4 (3.5 mm): 16" (40 cm) circular (cir) or straight.

Size U.S. 5 (3.75 mm): 16" (40 cm) cir or straight.

Adjust needle sizes if necessary to obtain correct gauge.

Notions
Stitch markers (m); stitch holder; tapestry needle.

Gauge
22½ sts and 36 rows = 4" (10 cm) over garter rib with larger needles, blocked.

25 sts and 30 rows = 4" (10 cm) over color chart with larger needles, blocked.

Knitting Knowledge

This project is worked flat and requires:
- Knitting with circular needles
- Casting on and binding off
- Reading charts
- Knitting and purling
- Increasing and decreasing
- Working stranded colorwork
- Locking floats
- Finishing

BACK

Cast on

With smaller needles and MC, CO 98 (110, 122, 130, 142) sts using the German twisted method (Techniques, page 141).

ROW 1: (RS) K1, k1 tbl, *p2, k2 tbl; rep from * to last 4 sts, p2, k1 tbl, k1.

ROW 2: (WS) P1, p1 tbl, *k2, p2 tbl; rep from * to last 4 sts, k2, p1 tbl, p1.

Rep last 2 rows until piece measures 2½ (2½, 2½, 2¾, 3)" (6.5 [6.5, 6.5, 7, 7.5] cm), ending with a WS row.

Switch to larger needles.

NEXT ROW: (RS) Knit.

NEXT ROW: (WS) P2, *k2, p2; rep from * to end of row.

These two rows form the pattern. Rep last 2 rows until piece measures 16 (16½, 17½, 17½, 17½)" (40.5 [42, 44.5, 44.5, 44.5] cm) from CO, ending with a WS row.

Shape armholes

BO 4 (6, 6, 7, 9) sts at beg of next 2 rows, then 2 sts at beg of next 0 (2, 2, 4, 4) rows—90 (94, 106, 108, 116) sts rem.

Dec 1 st at each end every RS row 2 (1, 2, 1, 2) time(s)—86 (92, 102, 106, 112) sts rem.

Cont even until armhole measures 7¾ (8, 8¾, 9½, 9¾)" (19.5 [20.5, 22, 24, 25] cm), ending with a WS row.

Shape shoulders

BO 7 (8, 9, 9, 10) sts at beg of next 6 rows—44 (44, 48, 52, 52) sts rem.

BO rem sts in patt. Cut yarn, leaving a 6" (15 cm) tail.

FRONT

With smaller needles and MC, CO 98 (110, 122, 130, 142) sts using the German twisted method.

ROW 1: (RS) K1, k1 tbl, *p2, k2 tbl; rep from * to last 4 sts, p2, k1 tbl, k1.

ROW 2: (WS) P1, p1 tbl, *k2, p2 tbl; rep from * to last 4 sts, k2, p1 tbl, p1.

Rep last 2 rows until piece measures 2½ (2½, 2½, 2¾, 3)" (6.5 [6.5, 6.5, 7, 7.5] cm) from CO, ending with a RS row.

Switch to larger needles. Join CC.

NEXT ROW: (WS) Purl and inc 1 st at center of row—99 (111, 123, 131, 143) sts.

Begin chart

NEXT ROW: (RS) Beg Row 1 at arrow for your size on chart and work 22 (28, 34, 38, 44) sts to left side of chart, beg at right side of chart and work 52-st rep once, then beg at right side of chart and work next 25 (31, 37, 41, 47) sts once more.

NEXT ROW: (WS) Beg Row 2 at arrow for your size on chart and work 25 (31, 37, 41, 47) sts to right side of chart, beg at left side of chart and work 52-st rep once, then beg at left side of chart and work last 22 (28, 34, 38, 44) sts once more.

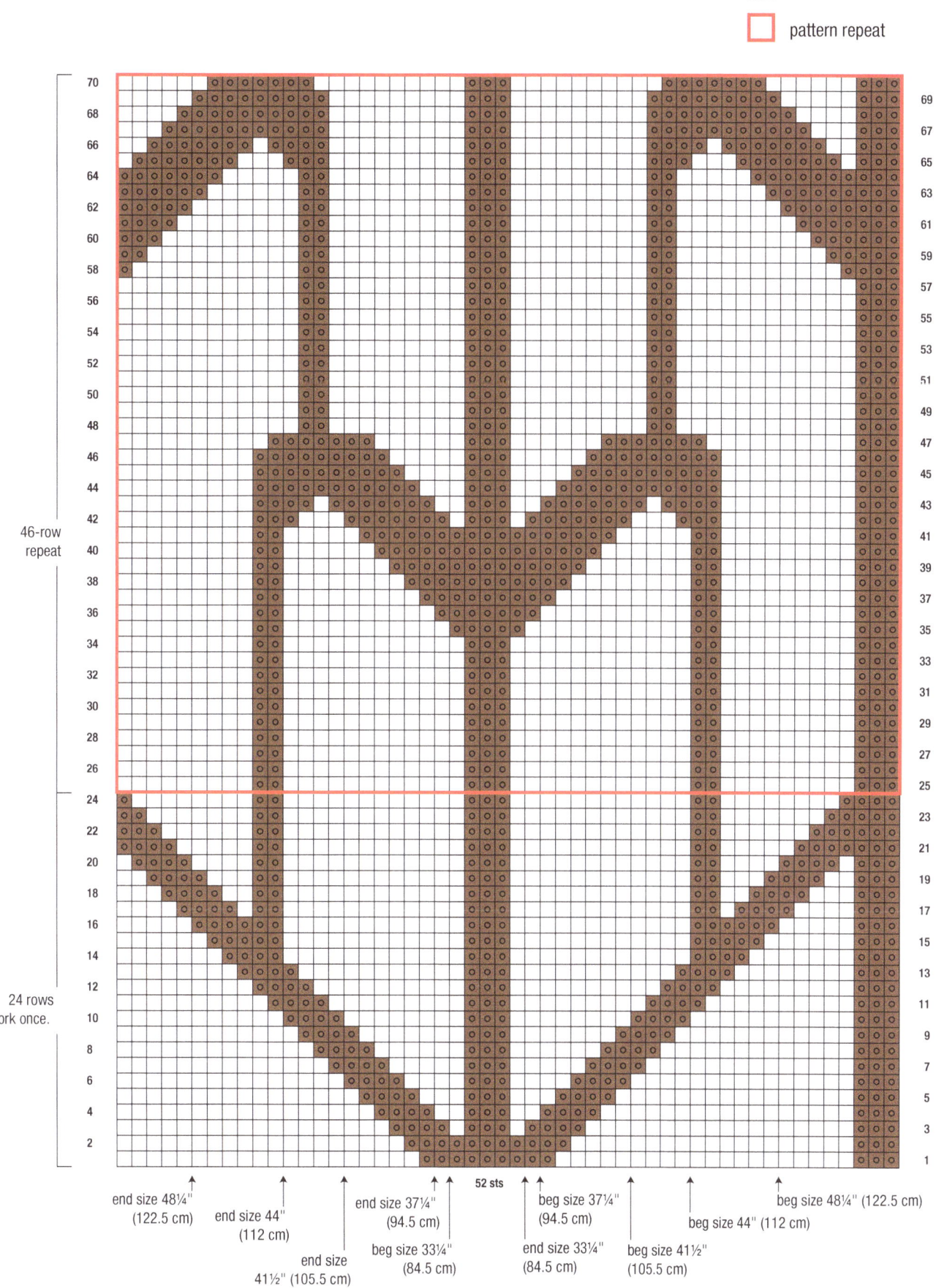

Brandt Pullover 29

Work chart Rows 3–70 as established, then rep Rows 25–70 until piece measures 16 (16½, 17½, 17½, 17½)" (40.5 [42, 44.5, 44.5, 44.5] cm) from CO, ending with a WS row.

Shape armholes

BO 4 (6, 6, 8, 10) sts at beg of next 2 rows, then 2 sts at beg of next 0 (2, 2, 4, 4) rows—91 (95, 107, 107, 115) sts rem.

Dec 1 st at each end of next 2 (1, 2, 1, 2) RS row(s)—87 (93, 103, 105, 111) sts rem.

Cont even until armhole measures 6 (6¼, 7, 7¾, 7¾)" (15 [16, 18, 19.5, 19.5] cm), ending with a WS row.

Shape neck

NEXT ROW: (RS) Work 34 (36, 41, 41, 45) sts in patt, BO next 19 (21, 21, 23, 23) sts for neck, work to end—34 (36, 41, 41, 44) sts rem for each shoulder.

Place sts for left shoulder on holder.

RIGHT SHOULDER

Cont in established patt and dec 1 st at neck edge every row 10 (10, 11, 11, 12) times—24 (26, 30, 30, 32) sts rem.

Work even until armhole measures 7¾ (8, 8¾, 9½, 9¾)" (19.5 [20.5, 22, 24, 25] cm), ending with a RS row.

BO at beg of every WS row 7 (8, 9, 9, 10) sts 3 times—3 (2, 3, 3, 2) sts rem.

BO rem sts. Cut yarn, leaving a 6" (15 cm) tail.

LEFT SHOULDER

Return held 34 (36, 41, 41, 44) sts to larger cir needle. With WS facing, join a ball of both colors at neck edge.

Cont in established patt and dec 1 st at neck edge every row 10 (10, 11, 11, 12) times—24 (26, 30, 30, 32) sts rem.

Work even until armhole measures 7¾ (8, 8¾, 9½, 9¾)" (19.5 [20.5, 22, 24, 25] cm), ending with a WS row.

BO at beg of RS rows 7 (8, 9, 9, 10) sts 3 times—3 (2, 3, 3, 2) sts rem.

BO rem sts. Cut yarn, leaving a 6" (15 cm) tail.

SLEEVES

With smaller needles and MC, CO 42 (46, 48, 50, 54) sts using the German twisted method.

ROW 1: (RS) K1, [k1 tbl] 1 (1, 0, 1, 1) time(s), *p2, k2 tbl; rep from * to last 4 (4, 3, 4, 4) sts, p2, [k1 tbl] 1 (1, 0, 1, 1) time(s), k1.

ROW 2: (WS) P1, [p1 tbl] 1 (1, 0, 1, 1) time(s), *k2, p2 tbl; rep from * to last 4 (4, 3, 4, 4) sts, k2, [p1 tbl] 1 (1, 0, 1, 1) time(s), p1.

Rep last 2 rows until piece measures 2" (5 cm) from CO, ending with a WS row.

Switch to larger needles.

NEXT ROW: (RS) Knit.

NEXT ROW: (WS) P0 (0, 1, 0, 0), *p2, k2; rep from * to last 0 (0, 1, 0, 0) st, p0 (0, 1, 0, 0).

INC ROW: (RS) Knit and inc 1 (1, 0, 1, 1) st each end of row—44 (48, 48, 52, 56) sts.

NEXT ROW: (WS) P2, place marker (pm), p1, *k2, p2; rep from * to last 5 sts, k2, p1, pm, p2.

Keeping first 2 and last 2 sts in St st (knit on RS rows, purl on WS rows), work 11 (11, 9, 7, 7) rows even in established patt.

INC ROW: (RS) K2, sm, m1, work in established patt to last 2 sts, m1, sm, k2—2 sts inc'd.

Rep inc row every 12 (12, 10, 8, 8) rows 10 (5, 7, 14, 14) more times, then every 0 (10, 8, 6, 6) rows 0 (6, 7, 4, 5) times—66 (72, 78, 90, 96) sts. Work new sts into patt.

Cont even until piece measures 18 (18½, 19, 19½, 20½)" (45.5 [47, 48.5, 49.5, 52] cm) from CO, ending with a WS row.

Shape sleeve cap

BO 4 (6, 6, 8, 10) sts at beg of next 2 rows, then 2 sts at beg of next 2 (2, 2, 4, 4) rows—54 (56, 62, 66, 68) sts rem.

Dec 1 st at each end of every RS row 18 (18, 18, 19, 17) times, then every row 4 (4, 6, 6, 8) times—10 (12, 14, 16, 18) sts rem.

BO rem sts. Cut yarn, leaving a 6" (15 cm) tail.

FINISHING

Weave in ends, waiting to cut yarn tails until after piece has been blocked. Block pieces to finished measurements. Join shoulders using mattress stitch (see Techniques). Set in sleeves. Sew side and sleeve seams using mattress stitch.

Work neckband

With smaller needles, MC and with RS facing, pick up and k38 (40, 42, 44, 46) sts along back neck edge, 20 (20, 21, 21, 24) sts along left front neck, 18 (20, 20, 22, 22) sts along front neck edge, then 20 (20, 21, 21, 24) sts along right front neck—96 (100, 104, 108, 116) sts. Pm for beg of rnd, and join for working in rnds.

RND 1: *K2, p2; rep from *.

Rep last rnd until neckband measures 1" (2.5 cm).

BO all sts loosely in patt. Cut yarn, leaving a 6" (15 cm) tail.

Weave in rem ends.

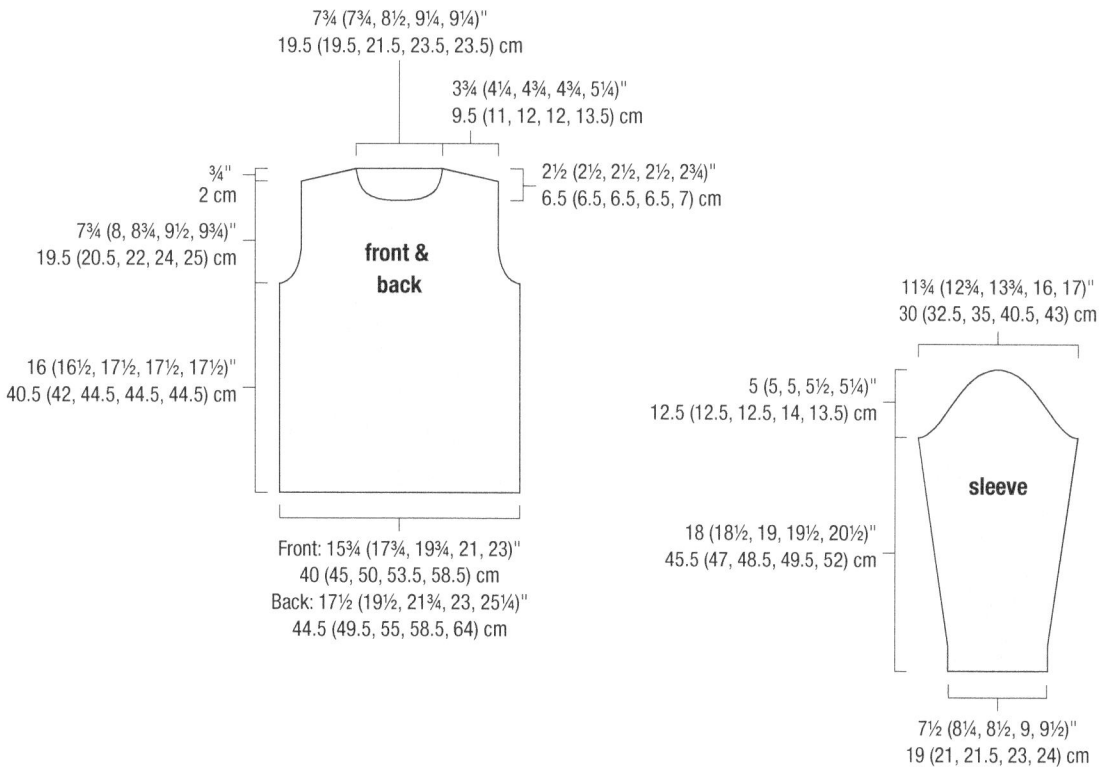

ARABELLA PULLOVER

Vertical repeating motifs are the epitome of Art Deco, the style I think of as the universal marker of urban architecture in the United States. Arabella is a luxurious garment featuring naturally dyed yarn made of alpaca, cashmere, and silk. Its body is filled with simple patterning, while each sleeve holds one strip of lacework down its center. The finished piece is warm, lightweight, and timeless.

Finished Size
30 (34, 38, 42, 46½, 50½)" (76 [86.5, 96.5, 106.5, 118, 128.5] cm) bust circumference and 21¼ (22¼, 22¾, 23½, 24, 24½)" (54 [56.5, 58, 59.5, 61, 62] cm) long.

Pullover shown measures 34" (86.5 cm) with 2¼" (5.5 cm) of ease.

Yarn
Fingering weight (#1 Super Fine).

Shown: A Verb for Keeping Warm Floating (70% alpaca, 20% cashmere, 10% silk; 400 yds [366 m]/100 g): Blush 3 (3, 4, 4, 4, 5) hanks.

Needles
Size U.S. 3 (3.25 mm): 16" (40 cm) circular (cir) and double-pointed (dpn).

Size U.S. 4 (3.5 mm): 16" (40 cm) cir and dpn.

Adjust needle sizes if necessary to obtain the correct gauge.

Notions
Stitch markers (m), including one in a unique color; stitch holder; tapestry needle.

Gauge
25 sts and 44 rows = 4" (10 cm) in patt on larger needles, blocked.

Knitting Knowledge
The body of this project is worked flat, and the sleeves are worked in the round to the armhole. It requires:

- Knitting with circular and double-pointed needles
- Casting on and binding off
- Reading lace charts
- Knitting and purling
- Increasing and decreasing
- Finishing

Notes
The ribbing sequence at the hem is set up so that the ribs line up with the pattern in the body of the garment. When shaping the back and the front, decrease or increase 2 stitches in from the edges.

STITCH GUIDE

Rib A: Panel of 6 sts
  Row 1: (WS) K2, p2, k2.
  Row 2: (RS) K6.
  Rep Rows 1 and 2 for patt.

Rib B: Panel of 13 sts
  Row 1: (WS) (P1, k1) 6 times, p1.
  Row 2: (RS) K13.
  Rep Rows 1 and 2 for patt.

BACK

Cast on

With smaller cir needle, CO 94 (107, 119, 132, 145, 158) sts using the German twisted method (Techniques, page 141).

FIRST ROW: (RS) Knit.

NEXT ROW: (WS) K0 (3, 3, 0, 3, 0), work Row 1 of Rib A (see Stitch Guide) over next 12 (6, 12, 12, 6, 6) sts, [Rib B (see Stitch Guide) over next 13 sts, Rib A over next 6 sts] 4 (5, 5, 6, 7, 8) times, work Rib A over next 6 (0, 6, 6, 0, 0) sts, k0 (3, 3, 0, 3, 0).

Rep last 2 rows until piece measures 2½" (6.5 cm), ending with a WS row.

Switch to larger cir needle.

Begin charts

SET-UP ROW: (RS) K0 (3, 3, 0, 3, 0), work Row 1 of Chart A 2 (1, 2, 2, 1, 1) time(s), Row 1 of Chart B 4 (5, 5, 6, 7, 8) times, Row 1 of Chart A 1 (0, 1, 1, 0, 0) time(s), k0 (3, 3, 0, 3, 0).

NEXT ROW: (WS) K0 (3, 3, 0, 3, 0), work Row 2 of Chart A 1 (0, 1, 1, 0, 0) time(s), row 2 of Chart B 4 (5, 5, 6, 7, 8) times, Row 2 of Chart A 2 (1, 2, 2, 1, 1) time(s), k0 (3, 3, 0, 3, 0).

Work Rows 3–8 of Chart B in established patt, then rep Rows 1–8, and rep Rows 1 and 2 of Chart A. *At the same time*, dec 1 st, 2 sts in from each end every 4 rows 6 times—82 (95, 107, 120, 133, 146) sts rem.

Work even for 2" (5 cm), ending with a WS row.

INC ROW: (RS) K2, m1, work to last 2 sts, m1, k2—2 sts inc'd.

Rep inc row every 6 rows 5 more times—94 (107, 119, 132, 145, 158) sts.

Cont even until piece measures 13¼ (13½, 13½, 13¾, 14, 14¼)" (33.5 [34.5, 34.5, 35, 35.5, 36] cm) from CO, ending with a WS row.

Shape armhole

BO 4 (6, 6, 6, 9, 10) sts at beg of next 2 rows, then 2 sts at beg of next 2 (2, 2, 4, 4, 6) rows—82 (91, 103, 112, 119, 126) sts rem.

Dec 1 st every RS row 0 (1, 1, 1, 4, 6) time(s)—82 (89, 101, 110, 111, 114) sts rem.

Cont even until armhole measures 7½ (8¼, 8¾, 9¼, 9½, 9¾)" (19 [21, 22, 23.5, 24, 25] cm), ending with a WS row.

NEXT ROW: (RS) K6 (7, 7, 8, 8, 8), work in established patt to end.

SHORT-ROW 1: (WS) P6 (7, 7, 8, 8, 8), work to last 5 (6, 6, 7, 7, 7) sts, w&t (see Techniques).

SHORT-ROW 2: (RS) K6 (7, 7, 8, 8, 8), work to last 5 (6, 6, 7, 7, 7) sts, w&t.

SHORT-ROW 3: (WS) P6 (7, 7, 8, 8, 8), work to last 10 (12, 12, 14, 14, 14) sts, w&t.

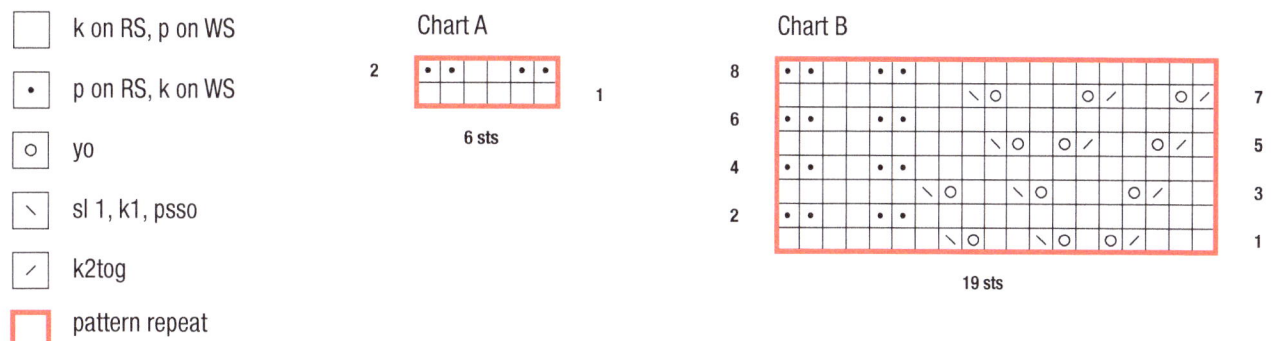

- ☐ k on RS, p on WS
- • p on RS, k on WS
- ○ yo
- \ sl 1, k1, psso
- / k2tog
- ☐ pattern repeat

SHORT-ROW 4: (RS) K6 (7, 7, 8, 8, 8), work to last 10 (12, 12, 14, 14, 14) sts, w&t.

SHORT-ROW 5: (WS) P6 (7, 7, 8, 8, 8), work to last 15 (18, 18, 21, 21, 21) sts, w&t.

SHORT-ROW 6: (RS) K6 (7, 7, 8, 8, 8), work to last 15 (18, 18, 21, 21, 21) sts, w&t.

NEXT ROW: (WS) Purl, picking up wraps and working them tog with the sts they wrap.

BO all sts in patt, picking up rem wraps and working them tog with the sts they wrap.

FRONT

Work as for back until armholes measure 5 (5½, 5¾, 6, 6¼, 6½)" (12.5 [14, 14.5, 15, 16, 16.5] cm), ending with a WS row.

Shape left shoulder

NEXT ROW: (RS) Work 31 (35, 38, 42, 43, 43) sts in established patt, turn, leaving rem 51 (54, 63, 68, 68, 71) sts on holder.

Dec 1 at neck edge every row 10 (12, 12, 12, 12, 12) times—21 (23, 26, 30, 31, 31) sts rem.

Work even until armhole measures 7½ (8¼, 8¾, 9¼, 9½, 9¾)" (19 [21, 22, 23.5, 24, 25] cm), ending with a WS row.

NEXT ROW: (RS) K6 (7, 7, 8, 8, 8) sts, work in established patt to end of row.

SHORT-ROW 1: (WS) Work to last 5 (6, 6, 7, 7, 7) sts, w&t.

NEXT ROW: (RS) K6 (7, 7, 8, 8, 8) sts, work to end of row.

SHORT-ROW 2: (WS) Work to last 10 (12, 12, 14, 14, 14) sts, w&t.

NEXT ROW: (RS) K6 (7, 7, 8, 8, 8) sts, work to end of row.

SHORT-ROW 3: (WS) Work to last 15 (18, 18, 21, 21, 21) sts, w&t.

NEXT ROW: (RS) Knit to end of row.

BO all sts in patt, picking up wraps and working them tog with the sts they wrap. Cut yarn, leaving a 6" (15 cm) tail.

Shape right shoulder

With RS facing, rejoin yarn at neck edge, k20 (19, 25, 26, 25, 28) sts and place these sts on holder, work to end in established patt—31 (35, 38, 42, 43, 43) sts rem.

Dec 1 st at neck edge every row 10 (12, 12, 12, 12, 12) times—21 (23, 26, 30, 31, 31) sts rem.

Work even until armhole measures 7½ (8¼, 8¾, 9¼, 9½, 9¾)" (19 [21, 22, 23.5, 24, 25] cm), ending with a RS row.

NEXT ROW: (WS) P6 (7, 7, 8, 8, 8) sts, work in established patt to end of row.

SHORT-ROW 1: (RS) Work to last 5 (6, 6, 7, 7, 7) sts, w&t.

NEXT ROW: (WS) P6 (7, 7, 8, 8, 8) sts, work to end of row.

SHORT-ROW 2: (RS) Work to last 10 (12, 12, 14, 14, 14) sts, w&t.

NEXT ROW: (WS) P6 (7, 7, 8, 8, 8) sts, work to end of row.

SHORT-ROW 3: (RS) Work to last 15 (18, 18, 21, 21, 21) sts, w&t.

NEXT ROW: (WS) Purl to end of row.

BO all sts in patt, picking up wraps and working them tog with the sts they wrap. Cut yarn, leaving a 6" (15 cm) tail.

SLEEVES

Note: The sleeves are made up of a lace panel centered in a field of garter rib.

With smaller dpn, CO 38 (44, 48, 52, 58, 62) sts using the German twisted method. Place marker (pm) for beg of rnd, and join for working in rnds, being careful not to twist sts.

Work in K1, P1 Rib (see Techniques) for 2" (5 cm). Change to larger dpn.

INC RND: Knit and inc 1 (3, 3, 3, 1, 1) st(s) evenly spaced—39 (47, 51, 55, 59, 63) sts.

NEXT RND: K1 (1, 3, 1, 3, 1), [p2, k2] 3 (4, 4, 5, 5, 6) times, pm, work first 13 sts of Row 1 of Chart B, pm, [k2, p2] 3 (4, 4, 5, 5, 6) times, k1 (1, 3, 1, 3, 1).

NEXT RND: Knit to m, sm, work first 13 sts of Row 2 of Chart B, sm, knit to end.

Cont in established patt. *At the same time*, inc 1 st 2 sts from each end every 11 (11, 10, 9, 9, 8) rnds 13 (14, 16, 18, 19, 21) times—65 (75, 83, 91, 97, 105) sts.

Work even until piece measures 16½ (17, 17, 17½, 18, 18¼)" (42 [43, 43, 44.5, 45.5, 46.5] cm).

Shape sleeve cap
Beg working back and forth, removing beg-of-rnd m.

BO 4 (5, 6, 6, 8, 9) sts at beg of next 2 rows, then 2 sts at beg of next 2 (2, 2, 4, 4, 6) rows—53 (61, 67, 71, 73, 75) sts rem.

Dec 1 st at each end every RS row 13 (15, 17, 18, 19, 19) times, then every row 4 (5, 6, 7, 8, 9) times—19 (21, 21, 21, 19, 19) sts rem.

BO rem sts. Cut yarn, leaving a 6" (15 cm) tail.

FINISHING

Weave in ends, waiting to cut yarn tails until after piece has been blocked. Block pieces to finished measurements. Using mattress stitch (see Techniques), join shoulders, sew in sleeves, then join side and sleeve seams.

Work neckband
With smaller cir needle and RS facing, pick up and k40 (45, 47, 50, 51, 52) sts along back neck edge, 20 (22, 24, 25, 26, 26) sts along left front neck, k20 (19, 25, 26, 25, 28) held sts at front neck, then pick up and k20 (22, 24, 25, 26, 26) sts along right front neck—100 (108, 120, 126, 128, 132) sts. Pm for beg of rnd and join for working in rnds.

Work in K1, P1 Rib for ¾" (2 cm).

BO all sts loosely in patt. Cut yarn, leaving a 6" (15 cm) tail. Weave in rem ends.

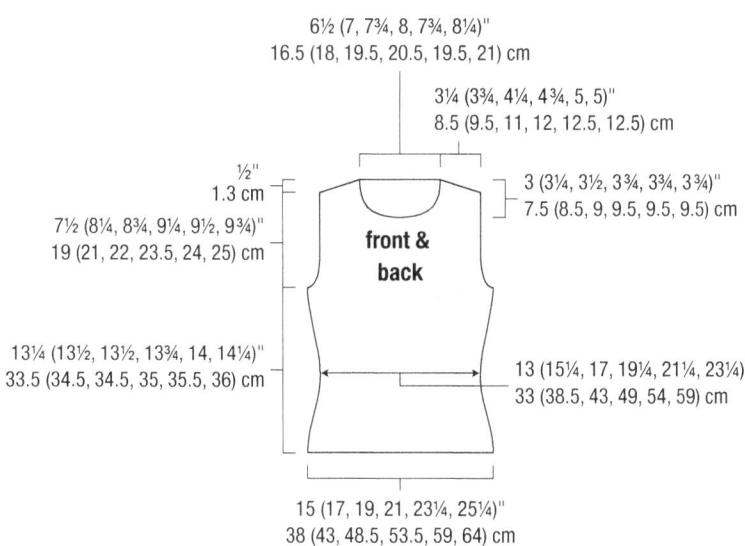

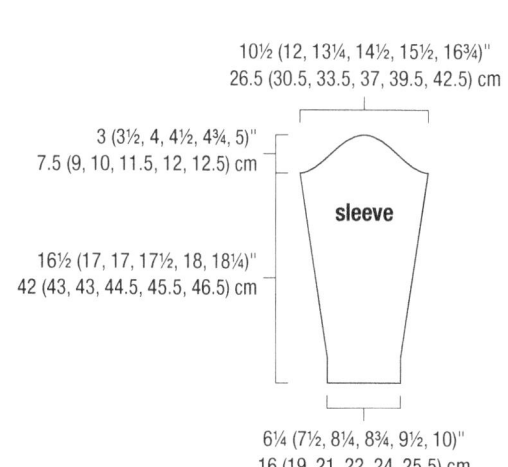

DECO CARDIGAN

This classically styled cardigan draws inspiration from a 1930s stained-glass light fixture with panes stacked in a cascading brick pattern. Placed at the sides and under the arm, the intarsia adds just a touch of drama. Want a little less contrast? Choose two shades of the same color for a subtler pattern.

Finished Size
34½ (38½, 42½, 47, 51, 55)" (87.5 [98, 108, 119.5, 129.5, 139.5] cm) chest circumference, including 1" (2.5 cm) overlap, and 23¼ (24¼, 25¾, 26¼, 27¾, 28¾)" (59 [61.5, 65.5, 66.5, 70.5, 73] long.

Cardigan shown measures 45½" (115.5 cm) with 1½" (3.8 cm) of ease.

Yarn
Worsted weight (#4 Medium).

Shown: Cascade Yarns 220 Heathers (100% Peruvian Highland wool; 220 yd [201 m]/100 g): #2448 Mallard (MC), 6 (7, 7, 8, 9, 9) skeins; #2440 Vinci (CC), 1 (1, 1, 1, 2, 2) skein(s).

Needles
Size U.S. 6 (4 mm): 24" (40 cm) and 40" (100 cm) or longer circular (cir) or straight.

Size U.S. 7 (4.5 mm): 16" (40 cm) cir or straight.

Adjust needle sizes if necessary to obtain correct gauge.

Notions
Stitch markers (m); tapestry needle.

Six ⅞" (22 cm) buttons.

Gauge
20 sts and 30 rows = 4" (10 cm) in St st with larger needles, blocked.

Knitting Knowledge

This project is worked flat and requires:
- Knitting with circular needles
- Casting on and binding off
- Reading charts
- Knitting and purling
- Working intarsia
- Knitting short-rows
- Knitting buttonholes
- Working duplicate stitch
- Finishing

Notes

Split CC into two balls, roughly equal in size, for working the two intarsia sections on the back and sleeves.

Read the instructions carefully when working this pattern so that the intarsia isn't interrupted by shaping.

BACK

Cast on

Using shorter smaller needle and MC, CO 90 (100, 110, 122, 132, 142) sts using the German twisted method (Techniques, page 141).

NEXT ROW: (WS) P2 (1, 2, 2, 1, 2), [k2, p2] to last 0 (3, 0, 0, 3, 0) sts, k0 (2, 0, 0, 2, 0), p0 (1, 0, 0, 0, 1, 0).

NEXT ROW: (RS) K2 (1, 2, 2, 1, 2), [p2, k2] to last 0 (3, 0, 0, 3, 0) sts, p0 (2, 0, 0, 2, 0), k0 (1, 0, 0, 0, 1, 0).

Cont in established ribbing until piece measures 2½" (6.5 cm), ending with a RS row.

Change to larger needles.

NEXT ROW: (WS) Purl. Cut yarn, leaving a 6" (15 cm) tail.

Begin Chart A

Note: Referring to Chart A, work stitches as specified in the instructions. The vertical and horizontal MC lines in the chart are worked in duplicate stitch.

SET-UP ROW: (RS) Join first ball of CC, k14, rejoin MC, knit to last 14 sts, join second ball of CC, k14.

NEXT ROW: P14 with CC, change to MC and twist yarns, purl to last 14 sts, change to CC and twist yarns, p14.

Following Chart A, work in St st (knit RS rows, purl WS rows) using intarsia method (see Techniques), cont as established until piece measures 11¼ (12½, 12½, 12½, 14, 14)" (28.5 [31.5, 31.5, 31.5, 35.5, 35.5] cm) from CO, ending with a WS row.

NEXT ROW: (RS) K9 with CC, change to MC and knit to last 9 sts, change to CC and k9.

Work 4 more rows as established.

NEXT ROW: (WS) P4 with CC, change to MC and purl to last 4 sts, change to CC and p4.

Work 4 more rows as established. Cut CC on both ends of work, leaving 6" (15 cm) tails.

Cont in St st with MC only until piece measures 14½ (15, 16, 16, 17, 17½)" (37 [38, 40.5, 40.5, 43, 44.5] cm), ending with a WS row.

Shape armholes

BO 4 (6, 6, 6, 8, 8) sts at beg of next 2 rows, 2 (2, 3, 4, 4, 4) sts at beg of next 2 rows, then 2 sts at beg of next 2 (2, 2, 4, 4, 4) rows—74 (80, 88, 94, 100, 110) sts rem.

Dec 1 st at each end of every RS row 0 (1, 1, 1, 2, 3) time(s)—74 (78, 86, 92, 96, 104) sts rem.

Cont even until armhole measures 8 (8½, 9, 9½, 10, 10½)" (20.5 [21.5, 23, 24, 25.5, 26.5] cm), ending with a WS row.

Shape shoulders

SHORT-ROWS 1 and 2: Work to last 7 (7, 8, 9, 9, 10) sts, w&t.

SHORT-ROWS 3 and 4: Work to last 14 (15, 17, 18, 18, 20) sts, w&t.

SHORT-ROWS 5 and 6: Work to last 22 (23, 26, 27, 28, 31) sts, w&t.

NEXT ROW: (RS) Knit, picking up wraps as you come to them and working them tog with the sts they wrap.

BO all sts. Cut yarn, leaving a 6" (15 cm) tail.

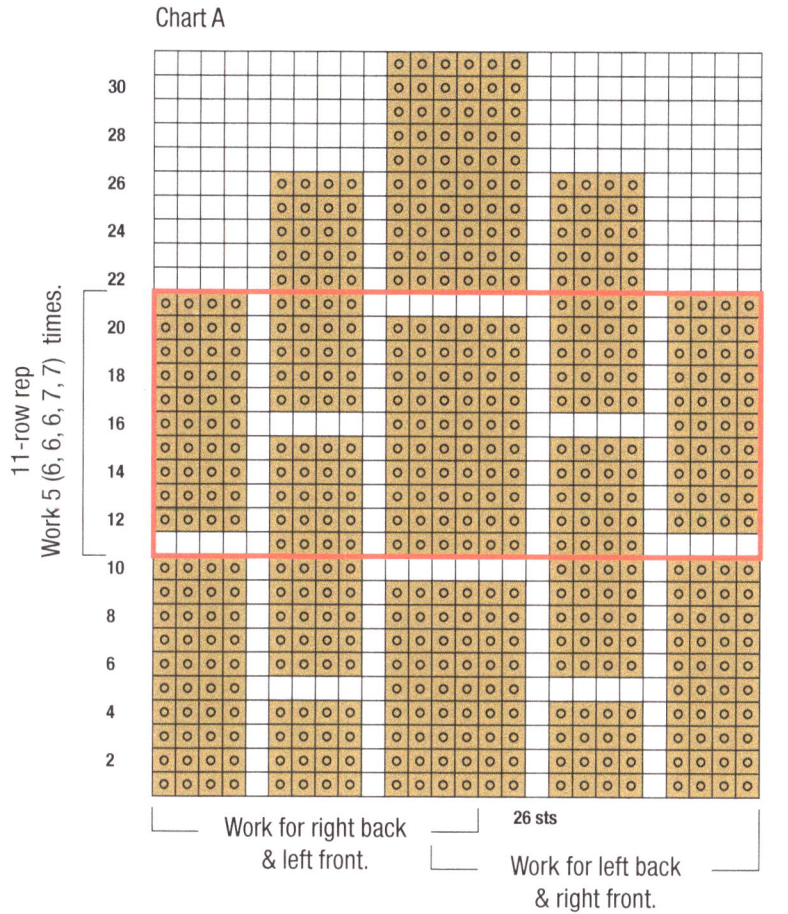

Chart A

Work 5 (6, 6, 6, 7, 7) times. 11-row rep

Work for right back & left front.

26 sts

Work for left back & right front.

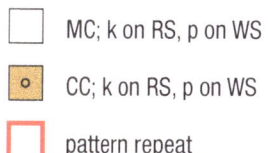

☐ MC; k on RS, p on WS

▣ CC; k on RS, p on WS

▢ pattern repeat

Note: Rows 1-26 of the chart show one-stitch vertical lines and short, horizontal rows of MC stitches. To make knitting easier (and the sides and sleeves less bulky), treat the intarsia section (see Techniques, page 141) as one solid block. Once each piece is made, duplicate stitch vertical and horizontal lines with MC to create the vertical and horizontal lines dividing up the CC section.

LEFT FRONT

Note: For Left and Right Fronts, work the chart only on the side of the garment (not at the buttonband).

Cast on

Using shorter smaller needle and MC, CO 42 (47, 52, 57, 62, 67) sts using the German twisted method.

NEXT ROW: (WS) P2 (2, 0, 1, 2, 3), [k2, p2] to last 0 (1, 0, 0, 1, 0) st(s), p0 (1, 0, 0, 1, 0).

NEXT ROW: (RS) K2 (3, 2, 2, 3, 2), [p2, k2] to last 0 (0, 2, 3, 0, 1) st(s), p0 (0, 2, 2, 0, 0), k0 (0, 0, 1, 0, 1).

Cont in established ribbing until piece measures 2½" (6.5 cm), ending with a RS row.

Change to larger needles.

NEXT ROW: (WS) Purl. Cut yarn, leaving 6" (15 cm) tail.

Begin Chart A

SET-UP ROW: (RS) Join CC and k14, rejoin MC and knit to end of row.

NEXT ROW: Purl to last 14 sts with MC, change to CC and twist yarns, p14.

Following Chart A, work in St st using intarsia method, cont as established until piece measures 11¼ (12½, 12½, 12½, 14, 14)" (28.5 [31.5, 31.5, 31.5, 35.5, 35.5] cm) from CO, ending with a WS row.

NEXT ROW: (RS) K9 with CC, change to MC and knit to end.

Work 4 more rows as established.

NEXT ROW: (WS) Purl to last 4 sts with MC, change to CC and p4.

Work 4 more rows as established. Cut CC, leaving a 6" (15 cm) tail.

Deco Cardigan

Cont in St st with MC only until piece measures 14½ (15, 16, 16, 17, 17½)" (37 [38, 40.5, 40.5, 43, 44.5] cm), ending with a WS row.

Shape armhole

BO at beg of RS rows 4 (6, 6, 6, 8, 8) sts once, 2 (2, 3, 4, 4, 4) sts once, then 2 sts 1 (1, 1, 2, 2, 2) time(s)—34 (37, 41, 43, 46, 51) sts rem.

Dec 1 st at beg of RS rows 0 (1, 1, 1, 2, 3) time(s)—34 (36, 40, 42, 44, 48) sts rem.

Shape neck

Dec 1 st at end of every other RS row 12 (13, 14, 15, 16, 17) times—22 (23, 26, 27, 28, 31) sts rem.

Cont even until armhole measures 8 (8½, 9, 9½, 10, 10½)" (20.5 [21.5, 23, 24, 25.5, 26.5] cm), ending with a RS row.

Shape shoulders

SHORT-ROWS 1 and 2: Work 15 (16, 18, 18, 19, 21) sts, w&t; work to end of row.

SHORT-ROWS 3 and 4: Work 8 (8, 9, 9, 10, 11) sts, w&t; work to end of row.

NEXT ROW: (WS) Purl, picking up wraps as you come to them and working them tog with the sts they wrap.

BO all sts. Cut yarn, leaving a 6" (15 cm) tail.

RIGHT FRONT

Cast on

Using shorter smaller needle and MC, CO 42 (47, 52, 57, 62, 67) sts using the German twisted method.

NEXT ROW: (WS) P2 (3, 2, 2, 3, 2), [k2, p2] to last 0 (0, 2, 3, 0, 1) st(s), k0 (0, 2, 2, 0, 0), p0 (0, 0, 1, 0, 1).

NEXT ROW: (RS) K2 (2, 0, 1, 2, 3), [p2, k2] to last 0 (1, 0, 0, 1, 0) st(s), k0 (1, 0, 0, 1, 0).

Cont in established ribbing until piece measures 2½" (6.5 cm), ending with a RS row.

Change to larger needles.

NEXT ROW: (WS) Purl.

Begin Chart A

SET-UP ROW: (RS) Knit to last 14 sts, join CC and knit to end of row.

NEXT ROW: P14 sts with CC, change to MC and twist yarns, purl to end.

Following Chart A, work in St st using intarsia method as established until piece measures 11¼ (12½, 12½, 12½, 14, 14)" (28.5 [31.5, 31.5, 31.5, 35.5, 35.5] from CO, ending with a WS row.

NEXT ROW: (RS) Knit to last 9 sts with MC, change to CC and twist yarns, knit to end of row.

Work 4 more rows as established.

NEXT ROW: (WS) P4 with CC, change to MC and purl to end of row.

Work 4 more rows as established. Cut CC, leaving a 6" (15 cm) tail.

Cont in St st with MC only until piece measures 14½ (15, 16, 16, 17, 17½)" (37 [38, 40.5, 40.5, 43, 44.5] cm), ending with a RS row.

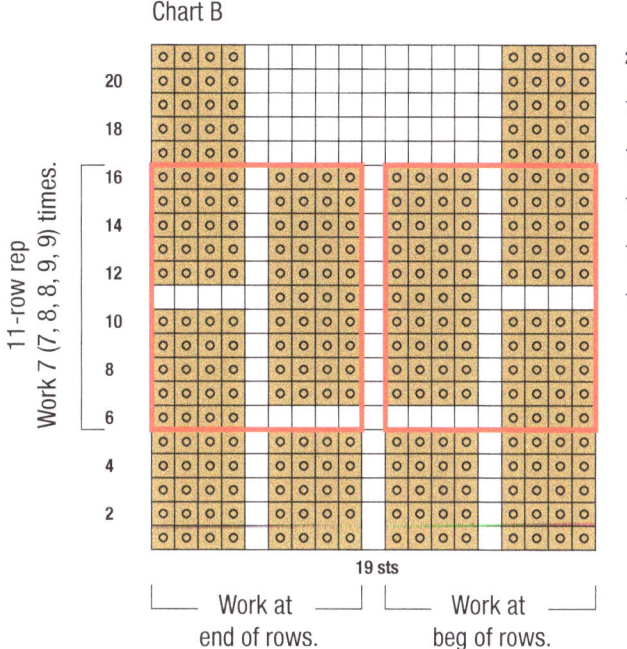

Shape armholes

BO at beg of WS rows 4 (6, 6, 6, 8, 8) sts once, 2 (2, 3, 4, 4, 4) sts once, then 2 sts 1 (1, 1, 2, 2, 2) time(s)—34 (37, 41, 43, 46, 51) sts rem.

Dec 1 st at end of RS rows 0 (1, 1, 1, 2, 3) time(s)—34 (36, 40, 42, 44, 48) sts rem.

Shape neck

Dec 1 st at beg of every other RS row 12 (13, 14, 15, 16, 17) times—22 (23, 26, 27, 28, 31) sts rem.

Cont even until armhole measures 8 (8½, 9, 9½, 10, 10½)" (20.5 [21.5, 23, 24, 25.5, 26.5] cm), ending with a WS row.

Shape shoulders

SHORT-ROWS 1 and 2: Work 15 (16, 18, 18, 19, 21) sts, w&t; work to end of row.

SHORT-ROWS 3 and 4: Work 8 (8, 9, 9, 10, 11) sts, w&t; work to end of row.

NEXT ROW: (RS) Knit, picking up wraps as you come to them and working them tog with the sts they wrap.

BO all sts. Cut yarn, leaving a 6" (15 cm) tail.

SLEEVES

Note: To keep CC section of patterning under the arm the same size throughout the sleeve, be sure to increase 2 stitches after changing to MC, using M1L at the beginning of the row and M1R at the end of the row (see Techniques).

Using shorter smaller needle and MC, CO 38 (40, 44, 48, 50, 54) sts using the German twisted method.

Work K2, P2 Ribbing (see Techniques) for 2" (5 cm), ending with a RS row.

Change to larger needles.

NEXT ROW: (WS) Purl. Cut yarn, leaving a 6" (15 cm) tail.

Begin Chart B

SET-UP ROW: (RS) Join a ball of CC, k9, rejoin MC and knit to last 9 sts, join a second ball of CC, k9.

NEXT ROW: (WS) P9 with CC, change to MC and twist yarns, purl to last 9 sts, change to CC and twist yarns, p9.

Work 2 more rows as established.

Deco Cardigan 43

INC ROW: (RS) K9 with CC, change to MC and twist yarns, k2, m1l, knit to last 11 sts, m1r, k2, change to CC and twist yarns, k9—2 sts inc'd.

Rep inc row every 6 rows 0 (0, 0, 10, 14, 9) times, every 8 rows 5 (12, 12, 5, 3, 8) times, then every 10 rows 5 (0, 0, 0, 0, 0) times—60 (66, 70, 80, 86, 90) sts.

Cont as established until piece measures 13 (13, 14½, 14½, 15¾, 15¾)" (33 [33, 37, 37, 40, 40] cm) from CO, ending with a WS row.

NEXT ROW: (RS) K4 with CC, change to MC and twist yarns, work to last 4 sts, change to CC and twist yarns, k4.

Work 4 more rows, and cont inc as established.

Cut CC, leaving 6" (15 cm) tails.

When inc are complete, cont even with MC only until piece measures 15½ (16, 16½, 17, 18, 19)" (39.5 [40.5, 42, 43, 45.5, 48.5] cm) from CO, ending with a WS row.

Shape sleeve cap

BO 4 (6, 6, 6, 8, 8) sts at beg of next 2 rows, 2 (2, 3, 4, 4, 4) sts at beg of next 2 rows, then 2 sts at beg of next 2 (2, 2, 4, 4, 4) row(s)—44 (46, 48, 52, 54, 58) sts rem.

Dec 1 st each end of every other RS row 11 (11, 12, 12, 13, 14) times, then every row 4 (4, 5, 6, 5, 6) times—14 (16, 14, 16, 18, 18) sts rem.

BO rem sts. Cut yarn, leaving a 6" (15 cm) tail.

FINISHING

Weave in all loose ends. With MC, and following chart as a guide, duplicate stitch (see Techniques) horizontal and vertical lines of pattern on sides, back, fronts, and sleeves.

Using mattress stitch (see Techniques) join shoulders. Sew in sleeves. Sew side and sleeve seams using yarn matching each section and lining up patt along edges.

Work buttonband

With longer smaller needle and MC, beg at lower right front edge, pick up and k123 (130, 137, 140, 145, 150) sts along right front edge to shoulder, 24 (26, 28, 30, 32, 34) along back neck edge, then 123 (130, 137, 140, 145, 150) sts along left front edge to bottom—270 (286, 302, 310, 322, 334) sts.

NEXT ROW: (WS) P2, [k2, p2] to end.

NEXT ROW: (RS) [K2, p2] to last 2 sts, k2.

Work 1 more row in established ribbing. Place markers for buttonholes along left front, placing bottom marker ¾" (2 cm) from bottom edge, next marker ½" (1.3 cm) above bottom rib, top marker at beg of neck shaping, then space rem 3 buttonholes evenly in between.

NEXT ROW: (RS) *Work in established ribbing to 2 sts before m, work buttonhole over next 3 sts (see Techniques); rep from * 5 more times, work to end of row—6 buttonholes worked.

Cont in established ribbing until band measures 1" (2.5 cm). BO all sts loosely in patt. Cut yarn, leaving a 6" (15 cm) tail.

Wait to trim yarn tails until after piece has been blocked.

Soak cardigan in cool water with a little wool wash. Lift out and gently squeeze to remove water. Lay work on a towel and roll up to remove excess water. Unroll, shape, and lay flat to dry. Trim yarn ends. Sew buttons to buttonband opposite buttonholes.

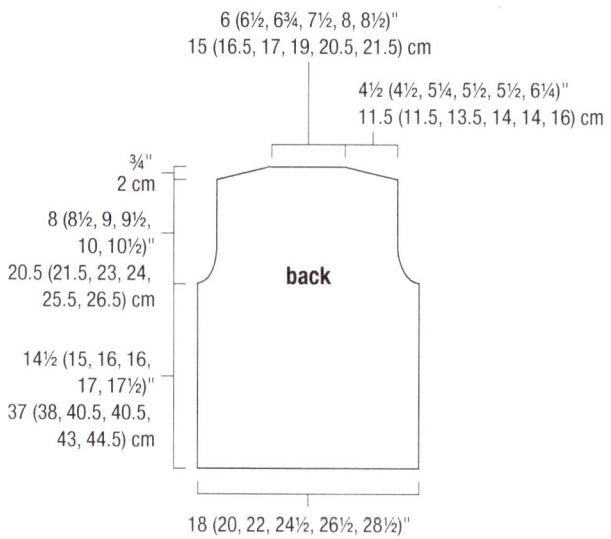

back

6 (6½, 6¾, 7½, 8, 8½)"
15 (16.5, 17, 19, 20.5, 21.5) cm

4½ (4½, 5¼, 5½, 5½, 6¼)"
11.5 (11.5, 13.5, 14, 14, 16) cm

¾"
2 cm

8 (8½, 9, 9½, 10, 10½)"
20.5 (21.5, 23, 24, 25.5, 26.5) cm

14½ (15, 16, 16, 17, 17½)"
37 (38, 40.5, 40.5, 43, 44.5) cm

18 (20, 22, 24½, 26½, 28½)"
45.5 (51, 56, 62, 67.5, 72.5) cm

sleeve

12 (13¼, 14, 16, 17¼, 18)"
30.5 (33.5, 35.5, 40.5, 44, 45.5) cm

7¼ (7¼, 7¾, 8¼, 8¾, 9¼)"
18.5 (18.5, 19.5, 21, 22, 23.5) cm

15½ (16, 16½, 17, 18, 19)"
39.5 (40.5, 42, 43, 45.5, 48.5) cm

7½ (8, 8¾, 9½, 10, 10¾)"
19 (20.5, 22, 24, 25.5, 27.5) cm

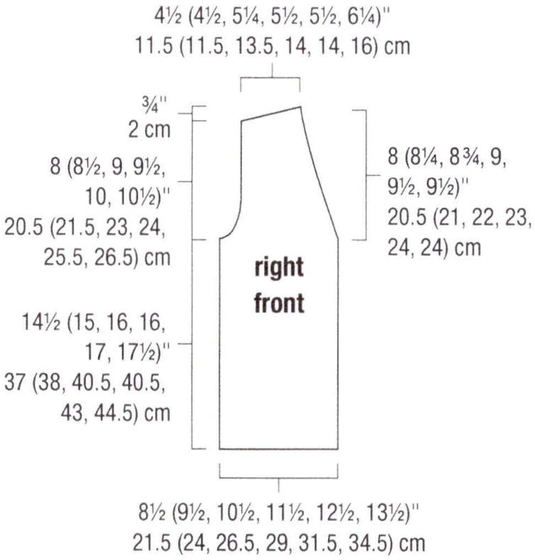

right front

4½ (4½, 5¼, 5½, 5½, 6¼)"
11.5 (11.5, 13.5, 14, 14, 16) cm

¾"
2 cm

8 (8½, 9, 9½, 10, 10½)"
20.5 (21.5, 23, 24, 25.5, 26.5) cm

8 (8¼, 8¾, 9, 9½, 9½)"
20.5 (21, 22, 23, 24, 24) cm

14½ (15, 16, 16, 17, 17½)"
37 (38, 40.5, 40.5, 43, 44.5) cm

8½ (9½, 10½, 11½, 12½, 13½)"
21.5 (24, 26.5, 29, 31.5, 34.5) cm

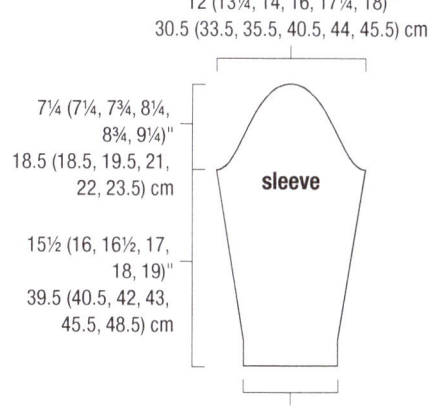

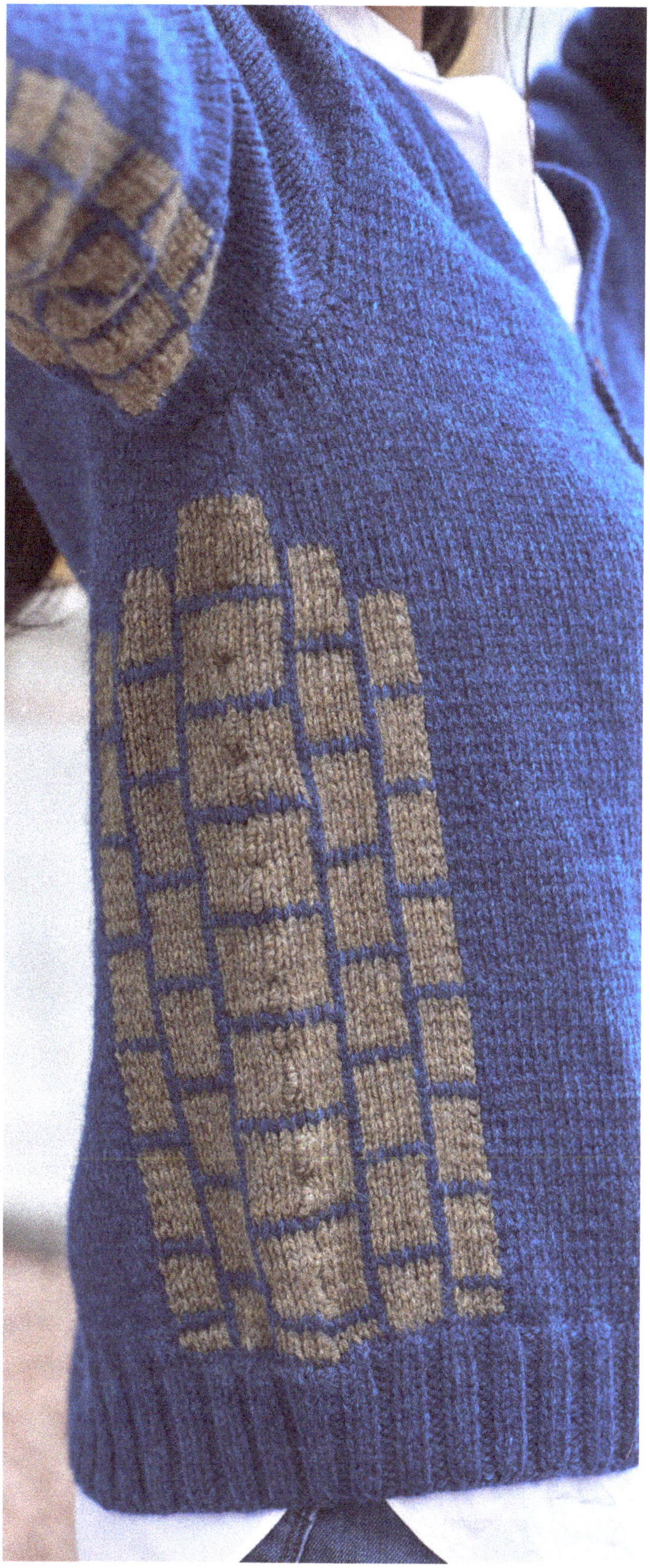

Deco Cardigan 45

EDWIN VEST

This vest is all about structure and symmetry. Beginning at the center, mirrored lines of traveling stitches angle, overlap, and intersect with each other. The cabled panels are separated by narrow stockinette-stitch columns. The back is also filled with these cables, and once assembled, the intersecting lines join together at the seams. My favorite detail has to be how the center column of stitches travels seamlessly into the collar.

Finished Size
34 (37½, 41½, 45, 48½)" (86.5 [95, 105.5, 114.5, 123] cm) chest circumference, and 26 (27½, 28, 28½, 29)" (66 [70, 71, 72.5, 73.5] cm) long.

Vest shown measures 41½" (105.5 cm) with 1" (2.5 cm) of positive ease.

Yarn
DK weight (#3 Light).

Shown: HiKoo Simplicity (55% superwash merino, 28% acrylic, 17% nylon; 117 yd [107 m]/50 g): #035 Turkish Coffee, 9 (10, 11, 12, 13) hanks.

Needles
Size U.S. 4 (3.5 mm): 24" (60 cm) circular (cir).

Size U.S. 3 (3.25 mm): 24" (60 cm) cir.

Adjust needle sizes if necessary to obtain the correct gauge.

Notions
Stitch markers (m); cable needle (cn); stitch holders; tapestry needle.

Gauge
30 sts and 33 rows = 4" (10 cm) in chart patt using larger needles, blocked.

Knitting Knowledge

This project is worked flat and requires:
- Knitting with circular needles
- Casting on and binding off
- Reading charts
- Knitting and purling
- Increasing and decreasing
- Cable knitting
- Finishing

STITCH GUIDE

1/1LC (1 over 1 left cross): Sl 1 st onto cn and hold in front, k1, k1 from cn.
1/1LPC (1 over 1 left purl cross): Sl 1 st onto cn and hold in front, p1, k1 from cn.
1/1RC (1 over 1 right cross): Sl 1 st onto cn and hold in back, k1, k1 from cn.
1/1RPC (1 over 1 right purl cross): Sl 1 st onto cn and hold in back, k1, p1 from cn.
2/1LC (2 over 1 left cross): Sl 2 sts onto cn and hold in front, k1, k2 from cn.
2/1LPC (2 over 1 left purl cross): Sl 2 sts onto cn and hold in front, p1, k2 from cn.
2/1RC (2 over 1 right cross): Sl 1 st onto cn and hold in back, k2, k1 from cn.
2/1RPC (2 over 1 right purl cross): Sl 1 st onto cn and hold in back, k2, p1 from cn.
2/2LC WS (2 over 2 left cross on wrong side): Sl 2 sts onto cn and hold in front, p2, p2 from cn.
2/2RC WS (2 over 2 right cross on wrong side): Sl 2 sts onto cn and hold in back, p2, p2 from cn.

BACK

Cast on
With smaller needle, CO 124 (140, 152, 168, 180) sts using the German twisted method (Techniques, page 141).

Work in K2, P2 Ribbing (see Techniques) for 2½" (6.5 cm), ending with a RS row.

Change to larger needles.

NEXT ROW: (WS) Work in rib as established and inc 3 (1, 3, 1, 1) st(s) evenly spaced—127 (141, 155, 169, 181) sts.

Begin charts
SET-UP ROW: (RS) K2, place marker (pm), working Row 1 of each chart, beg at arrow for your size on Chart A and work 6 (13, 20, 27, 33) sts to left side of chart, pm, k2, pm, work 52 sts of Chart B, pm, k3, pm, work 52 sts of Chart A, pm, k2, pm, work first 6 (13, 20, 27, 33) sts of Chart B, pm, k2.

NEXT ROW: (WS) P2, slip marker (sm), working Row 2 of each chart, beg at arrow for your size on Chart B and work 6 (13, 20, 27, 33) sts to right side of chart, sm, p2, sm, work 52 sts of Chart A, sm, p3, sm, work 52 sts of Chart B, sm, p2, sm, beg at left side of Chart A and work 6 (13, 20, 27, 33) sts to end of row.

Work Rows 3–79 in established patt, then rep Rows 12–79 until piece measures 16½ (17½, 17½, 17½, 17½)" (42 [44.5, 44.5, 44.5, 44.5] cm) from CO, ending with a WS row.

Shape armholes
BO 5 (6, 6, 7, 8) sts beg of next 2 rows, 2 (2, 3, 3, 4) sts beg of next 2 rows, then 2 sts beg of next 0 (2, 2, 4, 4) rows—113 (121, 133, 141, 149) sts rem.

Dec 1 st at each end of every RS row 3 (2, 5, 6, 8) times—107 (117, 123, 129, 133) sts rem.

Work even until armholes measure 8½ (9, 9½, 10, 10½)" (20.5 [23, 24, 25.5, 26.5] cm) from CO, ending with a WS row.

Shape shoulders
SHORT-ROWS 1 and 2: Work to last 10 sts, w&t.

SHORT-ROWS 3 and 4: Work to last 20 (20, 21, 20, 21) sts, w&t.

SHORT-ROWS 5 and 6: Work to last 30 (30, 31, 30, 31) sts, w&t.

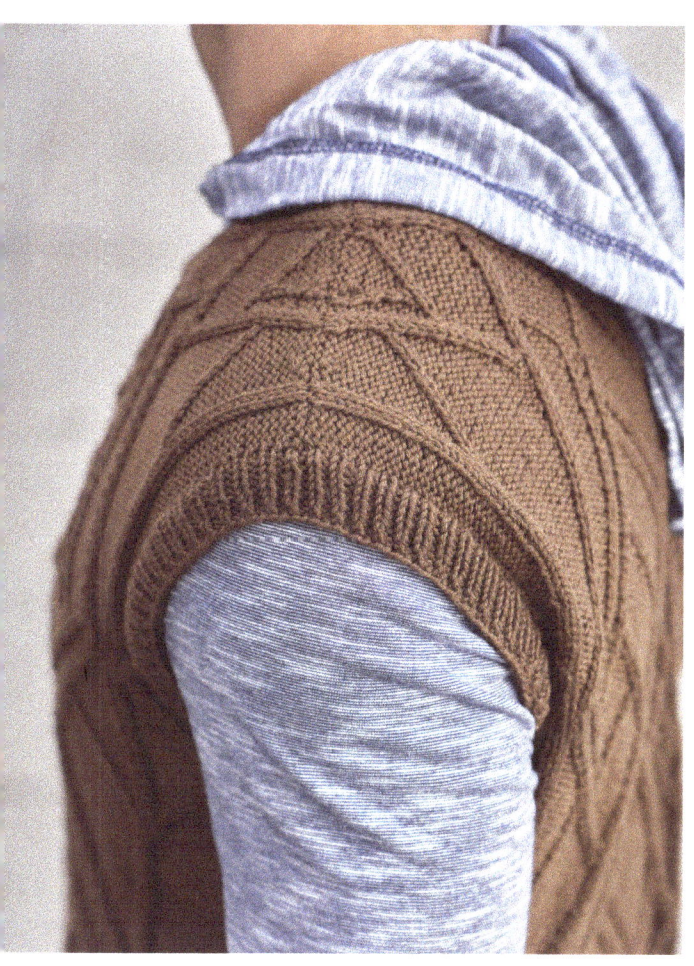

NEXT 2 ROWS: Work to end of row, picking up wraps and working them with the sts they wrap.

BO 33 (35, 36, 36, 36) sts, work until there are 41 (47, 51, 57, 61) sts on right-hand needle after BO, working sts as they appear, BO rem 33 (35, 36, 36, 36) sts.

Place center 41 (47, 51, 57, 61) sts on holder. Cut yarn, leaving a 6" (15 cm) tail.

FRONT

Work as for back until front measures 18 (19, 19½, 20, 20½)" (45.5 [48.5, 49.5, 51, 52] cm) from CO, ending with a RS row—107 (117, 123, 129, 133) sts rem. Mark center 3 sts.

NEXT ROW: (WS) Work 52 (57, 60, 63, 65) sts in patt as established and place sts on holder for right front, p3 and place these sts on holder for center front, then work rem 52 (57, 60, 63, 65) sts for left front.

Work left front

DEC ROW: (RS) Work in established patt to last 3 sts, k2tog, k1—1 st dec'd.

Rep dec row every RS row 18 (21, 23, 26, 28) more times—33 (35, 36, 36, 36) sts rem.

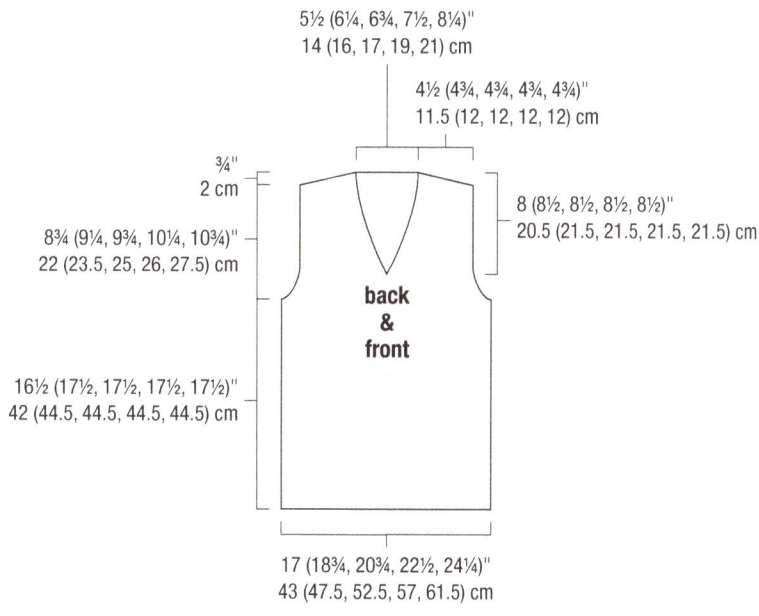

Edwin Vest

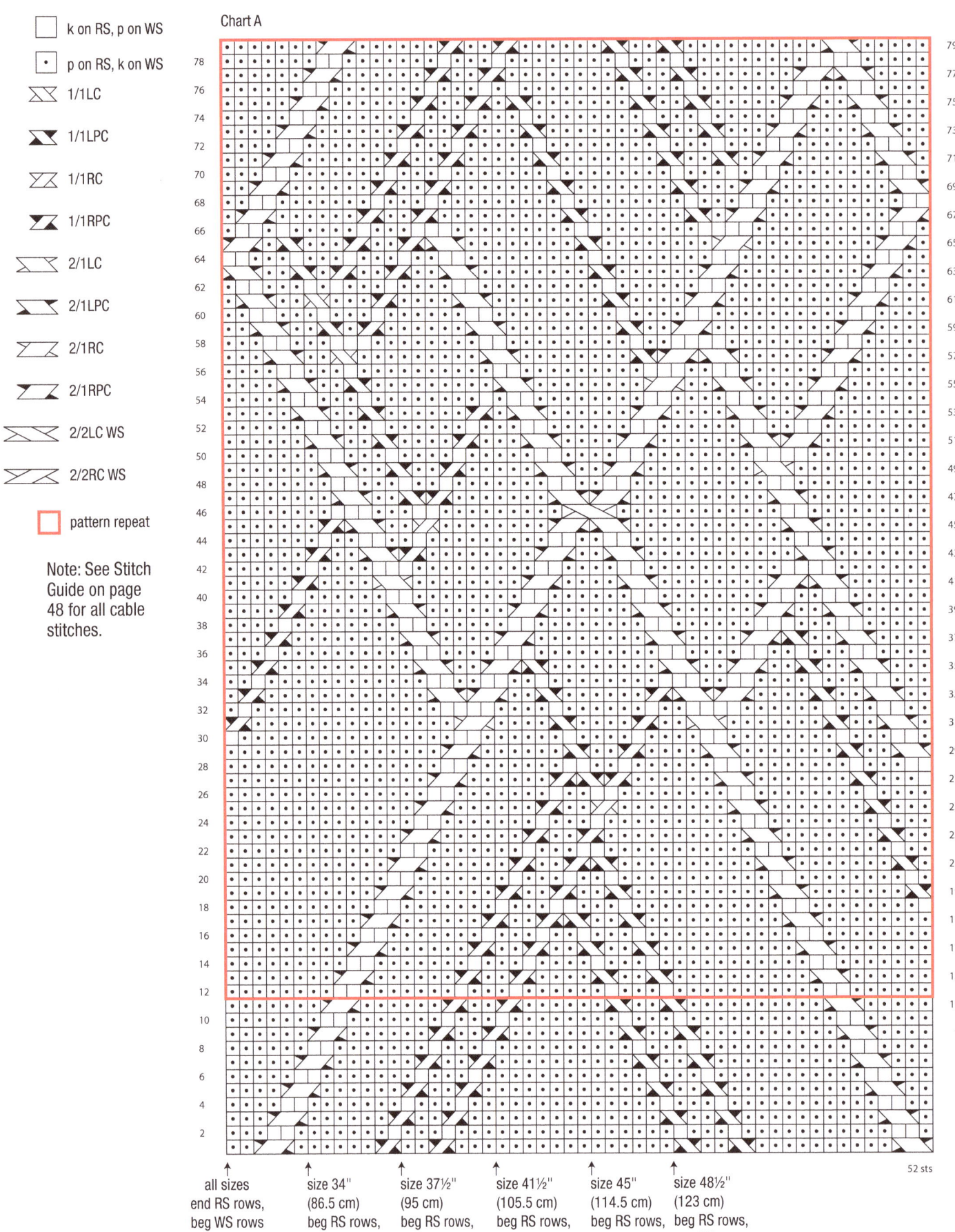

Chart B

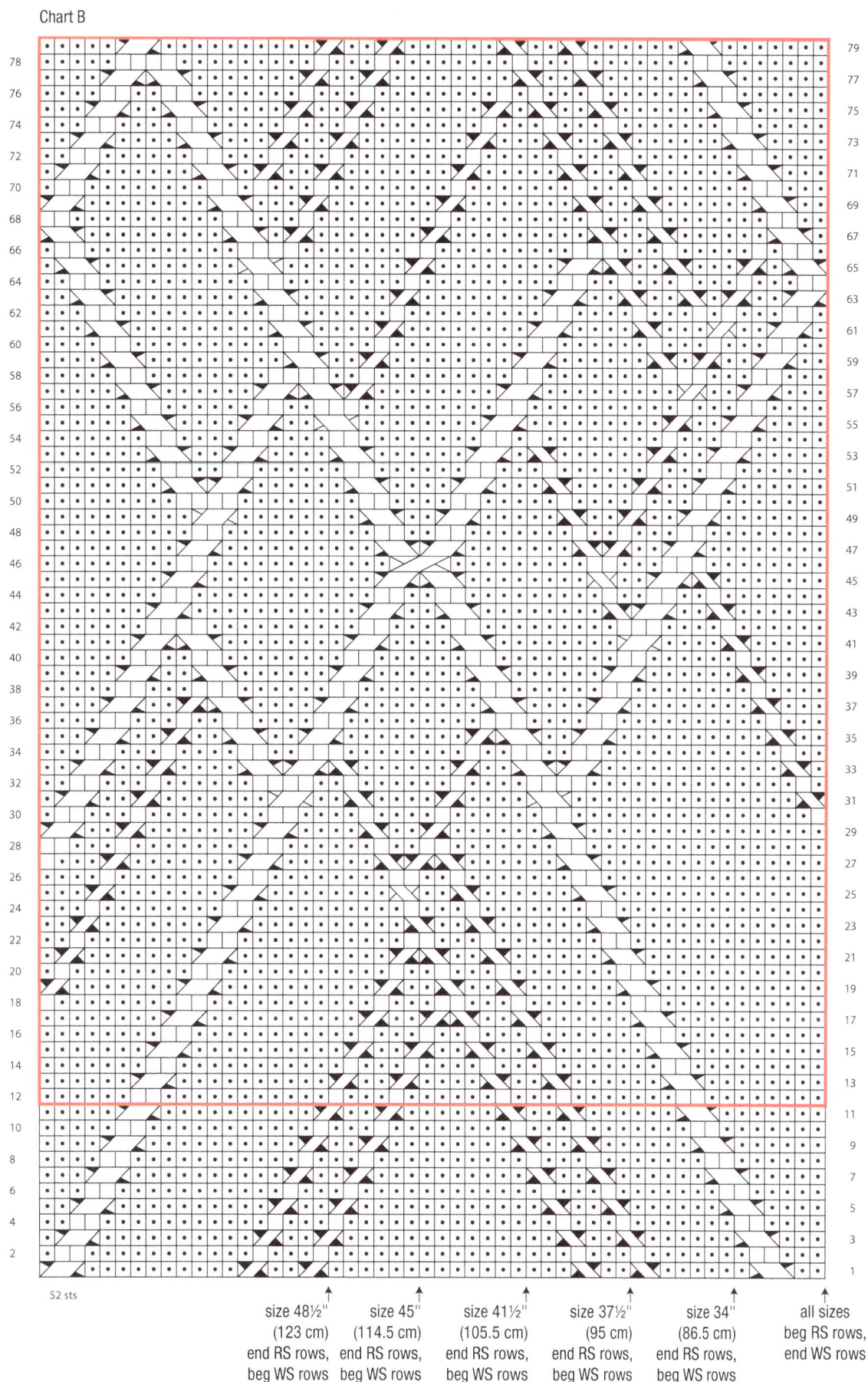

52 sts

size 48½" (123 cm) end RS rows, beg WS rows
size 45" (114.5 cm) end RS rows, beg WS rows
size 41½" (105.5 cm) end RS rows, beg WS rows
size 37½" (95 cm) end RS rows, beg WS rows
size 34" (86.5 cm) end RS rows, beg WS rows
all sizes beg RS rows, end WS rows

Edwin Vest

Cont even until armhole measures 8½ (9, 9½, 10, 10½)" (20.5 [23, 24, 25.5, 26.5] cm), ending with a RS row.

Shape shoulder

SHORT-ROWS 1 and 2: Work to last 10 sts, w&t; work to end of row.

SHORT-ROWS 3 and 4: Work to last 20 (20, 21, 20, 21) sts, w&t; work to end of row.

SHORT-ROWS 5 and 6: Work to last 30 (30, 31, 30, 31) sts, w&t; work to end of row.

NEXT ROW: (WS) Work to end of row, picking up wraps and working them tog with sts they wrap.

BO all sts. Cut yarn, leaving a 6" (15 cm) tail.

Work right front

Return held 52 (57, 60, 63, 65) right front sts to cir needle. With RS facing, rejoin yarn to beg with a RS row.

DEC ROW: (RS) K1, ssk, work in established patt to end—1 st dec'd.

Rep dec row every RS row 18 (21, 23, 26, 28) more times—33 (35, 36, 36, 36) sts rem.

Work even until armhole measures 8½ (9, 9½, 10, 10½)" (20.5 [23, 24, 25.5, 26.5] cm), ending with a WS row.

Shape shoulder

SHORT-ROWS 1 and 2: Work to last 10 sts, w&t; work to end of row.

SHORT-ROWS 3 and 4: Work to last 20 (20, 21, 20, 21) sts, w&t; work to end of row.

SHORT-ROWS 5 and 6: Work to last 30 (30, 31, 30, 31) sts, w&t; work to end of row.

NEXT ROW: (RS) Work to end of row, picking up wraps and working them tog with the sts they wrap.

BO all sts. Cut yarn, leaving a 6" (15 cm) tail.

FINISHING

Soak pieces in a bath of cool water with a little wool wash. Lift out and gently squeeze to remove water. Lay pieces on a towel and roll up to remove excess water. Lay pieces out to finished measurements and allow to dry completely.

Join shoulder and side seams using mattress stitch (see Techniques).

Work neckband

Note: The neckband and armholes are worked in the round.

With smaller cir needle and RS facing, beg at right shoulder seam, k41 (47, 51, 57, 61) held back sts, pick up and k58 (62, 62, 62, 62) sts along right neck, pm, k3 held front sts, then pick up and k58 (62, 62, 62, 62) sts along left neck—160 (174, 178, 184, 188) sts. Pm for beg of rnd and join to work in rnds.

DEC RND 1: [K1, p1] to 3 sts before m, k1, ssk, k3, k2tog, [k1, p1] to end of rnd—2 sts dec'd.

DEC RND 2: [K1, p1] to 2 sts before m, ssk, k3, k2tog, p1, [k1, p1] to end of rnd—2 sts dec'd.

Rep last 2 rnds until neckband measures 1" (2.5 cm).

BO all sts loosely in patt.

Work armholes

With smaller cir needle and RS facing, beg at bottom of armhole, pick up and k154 (164, 174, 184, 196) sts evenly along edge. Pm for beg of rnd and join to work in rnds.

Work in K1, P1 Ribbing (see Techniques) for 1" (2.5 cm).

BO all sts loosely in patt. Cut yarn, leaving a 6" (15 cm) tail.

Weave in all loose ends.

SAVOY CARDIGAN

Savoy is one of my favorite designs. I love how the coloring of the yarn shifts as it progresses up the garment and how its bold patterning demands attention. Charts detail the placement of each stitch. The fronts and back use the same chart, while the sleeves feature a centralized pattern surrounded by stripes. Because of Savoy's repeating pattern, it's actually easy to keep track of where you are in the chart once you begin.

Finished Size
30½ (34¼, 38½, 42¼, 46½, 50¾)" (77.5 [87, 98, 107.5, 118, 129] cm) bust circumference, with 1¼" (3.2 cm) overlap, and 25 (25¼, 25¼, 25½, 25¼, 25½)" (63.5 [64, 64, 65, 64, 65] cm) long.

Cardigan shown measures 34¼" (87 cm) with 2¼" (5.5 cm) of positive ease.

Yarn
Fingering weight (#1 Super Fine).

Shown: Shalimar Yarns Breathless (75% superwash merino, 15% cashmere, 10% silk; 420 yd [384 m]/100 g): Oyster (MC), 3 (3, 4, 4, 4, 5) hanks; Scarab (CC), 2 (2, 3, 3, 3 4) hanks.

Needles
Size U.S. 2 (2.75 mm): 24" (60 cm) and 40" (100 cm) circular (cir) or straight.

Size U.S. 3 (3.25 mm): 24" (60 cm) cir or straight.

Adjust needle sizes if necessary to obtain the correct gauge.

Notions
Stitch markers (m); tapestry needle.

Four ⅞" (22 mm) buttons.

Gauge
30 sts and 35 rows = 4" (10 cm) in chart patt with larger needles, blocked.

Knitting Knowledge

This project is worked flat and requires:
- Knitting with circular needles
- Casting on and binding off
- Reading charts
- Knitting and purling
- Increasing and decreasing
- Working stranded colorwork
- Locking floats
- Finishing

BACK

Cast on

Using shorter smaller cir or straight needles and MC, CO 118 (132, 148, 162, 178, 194) sts using the German twisted method (Techniques, page 141).

Work in K1, P1 Ribbing (see Techniques) for 2" (5 cm), ending with a RS row.

Change to larger needles.

NEXT ROW: (WS) Purl.

Begin charts

Note: Read RS rows of the charts from right to left and WS rows from left to right.

SET-UP ROW: (RS) Join CC, k2 with CC, place marker (pm), beg at arrow for your size with Row 1 on Chart B (page 59), work last 8 (15, 23, 30, 38, 46) sts of Chart B, pm, beg at right edge of Chart A and work 49 sts of chart, pm, beg at right edge of Chart B and work 49 sts of chart, pm, beg at right edge of Chart A and work 8 (15, 23, 30, 38, 46) sts, pm, k2 with CC.

NEXT ROW: (WS) P2 with CC, slip marker (sm), beg at arrow for your size with Row 2 of Chart A and work 8 (15, 23, 30, 38, 46) sts, sm, beg at left edge of Chart B and work Row 2, sm, beg at left edge of Chart A and work Row 2, sm, beg at left edge of Chart B and work 8 (15, 23, 30, 38, 46) sts, sm, p2 with CC.

Work Rows 3–80, then rep Rows 1–80 throughout. *At the same time*, shape waist.

Shape waist

DEC ROW: (RS) K2 with CC, sm, ssk, work in established patt to last 4 sts, k2tog, sm, k2 with CC—2 sts dec'd.

Rep dec row every 4 rows 9 more times, removing second and fourth marker for smallest size when those sts have been dec'd—98 (112, 128, 142, 158, 174) sts rem.

Work 4 rows even.

INC ROW: (RS) K2 with CC, sm, m1 with MC or CC to maintain chart patt, work in patt to last 2 sts, m1 with MC or CC to maintain patt, k2 with CC—2 sts inc'd.

Rep inc row every 6 rows 9 more times, and pm at each end for smallest size when a full 49-st rep can be worked at each end—118 (132, 148, 162, 178, 194) sts.

Cont even in established patt until piece measures 16½ (16½, 16, 16, 15½, 15½)" (42 [42, 40.5, 40.5, 39.5, 39.5] cm) from CO, ending with a WS row.

Shape armhole

BO 5 (5, 6, 8, 10, 12) sts at beg of next 2 rows, 2 (3, 3, 4, 5, 6) sts at beg of next 2 rows, then 2 sts at beg of next 0 (2, 4, 4, 6, 8) rows—104 (112, 122, 130, 136, 142) sts rem.

Cont even in established patt until armhole measures 7¼ (7½, 8, 8¼, 8½, 8¾)" (18.5 [19, 20.5, 21, 21.5, 22] cm), ending with a WS row.

Shape shoulders

SHORT-ROWS 1 and 2: Work to last 6 (8, 9, 9, 10, 10) sts, w&t.

SHORT-ROWS 3 and 4: Work to last 12 (16, 18, 18, 20, 20) sts, w&t.

SHORT-ROWS 5 and 6: Work to last 18 (24, 27, 27, 30, 30) sts, w&t.

SHORT-ROWS 7 and 8: Work to last 24 (33, 36, 38, 39, 40) sts, w&t.

NEXT ROW: (WS) P2 with CC, sm, beg at arrow for your size with Row 2 of Chart A and work 1 (8, 16, 23, 31, 39) st(s) sm, beg at left edge of Chart B and work Row 2, sm, p2 with CC.

Work Rows 3–80, then rep Rows 1–80 throughout. *At the same time*, shape waist and neck.

Shape waist and neck

DEC ROW: (RS) K2 sts with CC, sm, SSK, work in established patt to last 4 sts, ssk, sm, k2 with CC—1 st dec'd.

Rep dec row every 4 rows 9 more times, removing third marker for 2 smallest sizes when those sts have been dec'd—44 (51, 59, 66, 74, 82) sts rem.

Work 4 rows even.

NEXT ROW: (RS) K2 with CC, sm, ssk, work to last 2 sts, m1 in MC or CC to maintain patt, sm, k2 with CC—1 st dec'd for neck, and 1 st inc'd for bust.

Cont inc at end of every 6 rows 9 more times and dec at beg of every 4 rows 24 (27, 29, 31, 33, 35) more times until piece measures 16½ (16½, 16, 16, 15½, 15½)" (42 [42, 40.5, 40.5, 39.5, 39.5] cm) from CO, ending with a RS row.

Shape armhole

Cont established neck shaping, BO at beg of WS rows 5 (5, 6, 8, 10, 12) sts once, 2 (3, 3, 4, 5, 6) sts once, then 2 sts 0 (1, 2, 2, 3, 4) time(s)—22 (23, 26, 28, 29, 30) sts rem.

Cont even until armhole measures 7¼ (7½, 8, 8¼, 8½, 8¾)" (18.5 [19, 20.5, 21, 21.5, 22] cm), ending with a WS row.

Shape shoulders

SHORT-ROWS 1 and 2: Work to last 6 (6, 7, 7, 7, 8) sts, w&t, work to end of row.

SHORT-ROWS 3 and 4: Work to last 12 (12, 14, 14, 14, 16) sts, w&t, work to end of row.

SHORT-ROWS 5 and 6: Work to last 18 (18, 21, 21, 21, 24) sts, w&t, work to end of row.

NEXT ROW: (RS) Work to end of row, picking up wraps as you come to them and working them tog with the sts they wrap.

BO all sts in patt. Cut yarn, leaving a 6" (15 cm) tail.

NEXT 2 ROWS: Work to end of row, picking up wraps as you come to them and working them tog with the sts they wrap.

BO all sts in patt. Cut yarn, leaving a 6" (15 cm) tail.

RIGHT FRONT

Cast on

Using shorter smaller cir or straight needles and MC, CO 54 (61, 69, 76, 84, 92) sts using the German twisted method.

Work in K1, P1 Ribbing for 2" (5 cm), ending with a RS row.

Change to larger needles.

NEXT ROW: (WS) Purl.

Begin charts

SET-UP ROW: (RS) Join CC, k2 with CC, pm, beg at right edge of Chart B and work Row 1, pm, beg at right edge of Chart A and work Row 1 over next 1 (8, 16, 23, 31, 39) st(s), pm, k2 with CC.

Savoy Cardigan

☐ MC; k on RS, p on WS

○ CC; k on RS, p on WS

☐ pattern repeat

Chart A

49 sts

- end back size 50¾" (129 cm)
- end back size 46½" (118 cm)
- end back size 42¼" (107.5 cm)
- end back size 38½" (98 cm)
- end back size 34¼" (87 cm)
- end back size 30½" (77.5 cm)

- end left front all sizes
- end right front size 50¾" (129 cm)
- end right front size 46½" (118 cm)
- end right front size 42¼" (107.5 cm)
- end right front size 38½" (98 cm)
- end right front size 34¼" (87 cm)
- end right front size 30½" (77.5 cm)

58 URBAN KNIT COLLECTION

Chart B

Savoy Cardigan

LEFT FRONT

Cast on
Using shorter smaller cir or straight needles and MC, CO 54 (61, 69, 76, 84, 92) sts using the German twisted method.

Work in K1, P1 Ribbing for 2" (5 cm), ending with a RS row.

Change to larger needles.

NEXT ROW: (WS) Purl.

Begin charts
SET-UP ROW: (RS) Join CC, k2 with CC, pm, beg at arrow for your size with Row 1 of Chart B, work 1 (8, 16, 23, 31, 39) st(s), pm, beg at right edge of Chart A and work Row 1, pm, k2 with CC.

NEXT ROW: (WS) P2 with CC, sm, beg at left edge of Chart A and work Row 2, sm, beg at left edge of Chart B, work 1 (8, 16, 23, 31, 39) st(s), sm, p2 with CC.

Work Rows 3–80, then rep Rows 1–80 throughout. *At the same time*, shape waist.

Shape waist and neck
DEC ROW: (RS) K2 with CC, sm, k2tog, work in established patt to end—1 st dec'd.

Rep dec row every 4 rows 9 more times—44 (51, 59, 66, 74, 82) sts rem.

Work 4 rows even.

NEXT ROW: (RS) K2 with CC, sm, m1 with MC or CC to maintain patt, work to last 4 sts, k2tog, sm, k2 with CC—1 st dec'd for neck and 1 st inc'd for bust.

Cont inc at beg of every 6 rows 9 more times and dec at end of every 4 rows 24 (27, 29, 31, 33, 35) more times until piece measures 16½ (16½, 16, 16, 15½, 15½)" (42 [42, 40.5, 40.5, 39.5, 39.5] cm) from CO, ending with a RS row.

Shape armhole
Cont established neck shaping, BO at beg of RS rows 5 (5, 6, 8, 10, 12) sts once, 2 (3, 3, 4, 5, 6) sts once, then 2 sts 0 (1, 2, 2, 3, 4) time(s)—22 (23, 26, 28, 29, 30) sts rem when shaping is complete.

Cont even until armhole measures 7¼ (7½, 8, 8¼, 8½, 8¾)" (18.5 [19, 20.5, 21, 21.5, 22] cm), ending with a RS row.

Shape shoulder
SHORT-ROWS 1 and 2: Work to last 6 (6, 7, 7, 7, 8) sts, w&t, work to end of row.

SHORT-ROWS 3 and 4: Work to last 12 (12, 14, 14, 14, 16) sts, w&t, work to end of row.

SHORT-ROWS 5 and 6: Work to last 18 (18, 21, 21, 21, 24) sts, w&t, work to end of row.

NEXT ROW: (WS) Work to end of row, picking up wraps as you come to them and working them tog with the sts they wrap.

BO all sts in patt. Cut yarn, leaving a 6" (15 cm) tail.

SLEEVES

With shorter smaller cir or straight needles and MC, CO 44 (50, 56, 62, 68, 74) sts using the German twisted method.

Work in K1, P1 Rib for 2" (5 cm), ending with a RS row.

Change to larger needles.

NEXT ROW: (WS) Purl.

Begin charts
SET-UP ROW: (RS) Join CC, beg at arrow for your size with Row 1 of Chart C, work 44 (50, 56, 62, 1, 4) st(s), work 66-st rep 0 (0, 0, 0, 1, 1) time(s), then work first 0 (0, 0, 0, 1, 4) st(s) of chart again.

Work 5 (5, 3, 3, 3, 3) rows in established patt.

INC ROW: (RS) Work 2 sts in established patt, m1 with MC or CC to maintain patt, work to last 2 sts, m1 with MC or CC to maintain patt, work 2 sts—2 sts inc'd.

Rep inc row every 6 rows 17 (19, 14, 11, 12, 12) more times, then every 4 rows 0 (0, 7, 12, 13, 15) times—80 (90, 100, 110, 120, 130) sts. Work new sts in patt, and *at the same time*, cont through Row 97 of chart, then rep Rows 18–97 throughout.

Cont even until piece measures 16½ (17, 17, 17½, 18, 18¼)" (42 [43, 43, 44.5, 45.5, 46.5] cm) from CO, ending with a WS row.

Shape sleeve cap

BO 5 (5, 6, 8, 10, 12) sts at beg of next 2 rows, 2 (3, 3, 4, 5, 6) sts at beg of next 2 rows, 2 sts at beg of next 0 (2, 4, 4, 6, 8) rows—66 (70, 74, 78, 78, 78) sts rem.

Dec 1 st at each end of every RS row 20 times, then every row 2 (3, 3, 4, 4, 4) times—22 (24, 28, 30, 30, 30) sts rem.

BO rem sts in patt. Cut yarn, leaving a 6" (15 cm) tail.

FINISHING

Weave in all ends, waiting to cut yarn tails until after pieces have been blocked.

Join shoulders using mattress stitch (see Techniques). Sew in sleeves. Join side and sleeve seams using mattress stitch.

Work buttonband

With longer smaller cir needle and MC, with RS facing, beg at lower right front edge, pick up and k188 (192, 194, 194, 196, 196) sts along right front edge to shoulder, 40 (46, 50, 54, 58, 62) sts along back neck edge, then 188 (192, 194, 194, 196, 196) sts along left front edge to bottom edge—416 (430, 438, 442, 450, 454) sts.

Work in K1, P1 Ribbing for ½" (1.3 cm), ending with a WS row.

BUTTONHOLE ROW: (RS) Work 5 sts in established rib patt, *work buttonhole (see Techniques) over next 3 sts, cont in rib until there are 7 sts on right needle tip after buttonhole gap; rep from * 2 more times, work buttonhole over next 3 sts, then work in rib to end.

Cont in established rib patt until buttonband measures 1¼" (3.2 cm).

BO all sts loosely in rib patt. Cut yarn, leaving a 6" (15 cm) tail.

Soak cardigan in cool water with a little wool wash. Lift out and gently squeeze to remove water. Lay it on a towel and roll up to remove excess water. Unroll, shape, and lay flat to dry. Sew buttons to left front ribbing opposite buttonholes.

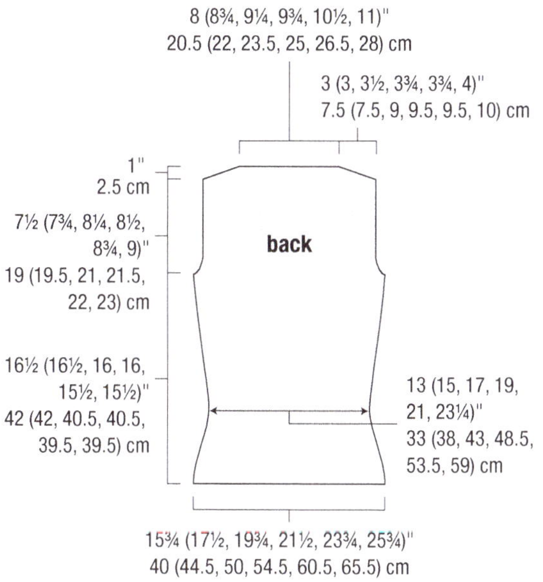

back

8 (8¾, 9¼, 9¾, 10½, 11)"
20.5 (22, 23.5, 25, 26.5, 28) cm

3 (3, 3½, 3¾, 3¾, 4)"
7.5 (7.5, 9, 9.5, 9.5, 10) cm

1"
2.5 cm

7½ (7¾, 8¼, 8½, 8¾, 9)"
19 (19.5, 21, 21.5, 22, 23) cm

16½ (16½, 16, 16, 15½, 15½)"
42 (42, 40.5, 40.5, 39.5, 39.5) cm

13 (15, 17, 19, 21, 23¼)"
33 (38, 43, 48.5, 53.5, 59) cm

15¾ (17½, 19¾, 21½, 23¾, 25¾)"
40 (44.5, 50, 54.5, 60.5, 65.5) cm

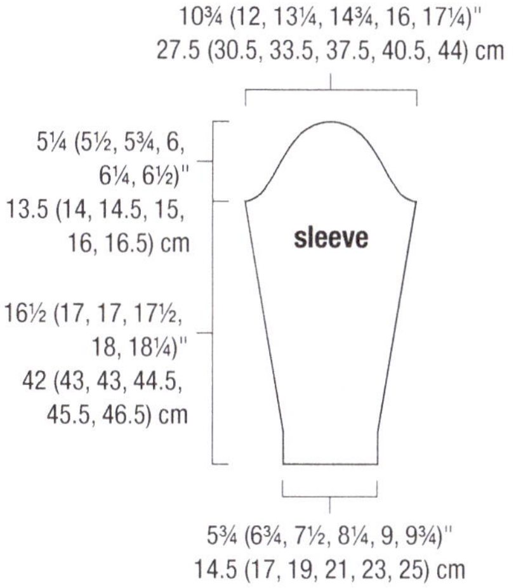

sleeve

10¾ (12, 13¼, 14¾, 16, 17¼)"
27.5 (30.5, 33.5, 37.5, 40.5, 44) cm

5¼ (5½, 5¾, 6, 6¼, 6½)"
13.5 (14, 14.5, 15, 16, 16.5) cm

16½ (17, 17, 17½, 18, 18¼)"
42 (43, 43, 44.5, 45.5, 46.5) cm

5¾ (6¾, 7½, 8¼, 9, 9¾)"
14.5 (17, 19, 21, 23, 25) cm

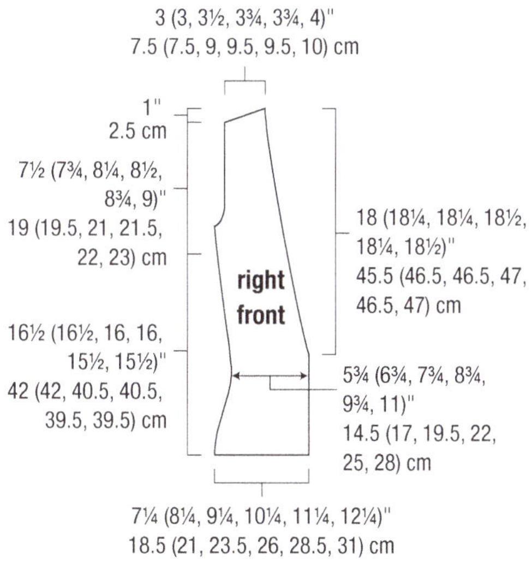

right front

3 (3, 3½, 3¾, 3¾, 4)"
7.5 (7.5, 9, 9.5, 9.5, 10) cm

1"
2.5 cm

7½ (7¾, 8¼, 8½, 8¾, 9)"
19 (19.5, 21, 21.5, 22, 23) cm

18 (18¼, 18¼, 18½, 18¼, 18½)"
45.5 (46.5, 46.5, 47, 46.5, 47) cm

16½ (16½, 16, 16, 15½, 15½)"
42 (42, 40.5, 40.5, 39.5, 39.5) cm

5¾ (6¾, 7¾, 8¾, 9¾, 11)"
14.5 (17, 19.5, 22, 25, 28) cm

7¼ (8¼, 9¼, 10¼, 11¼, 12¼)"
18.5 (21, 23.5, 26, 28.5, 31) cm

Savoy Cardigan 63

ROSEMA WRAP

The Rosema wrap is the kind of piece you'll reach for again and again—whether it's warding off a winter chill or keeping you cozy in overly air-conditioned spaces. Knit in a soft, luxurious merino, it features a simple lace and cable motif that's both engaging to work and effortlessly elegant to wear. The wrap is worked from side to side, with sleeves picked up from the body and knit downward, creating a fluid, seamless silhouette.

Finished Size
14 (16¼, 18¾)" (35.5 [41.4, 47.5] cm) across back at shoulders and 22¾ (22¾, 23¼)" (58 [58, 59] cm) long.

Wrap shown measures 14" (35.5 cm).

Yarn
Worsted weight (#4 Medium).

Shown: Hazel Knits Cadence (100% superwash merino; 200 yd [183 m]/100 g): Sassafras, 9 (9, 10) hanks.

Needles
Size U.S. 6 (4 mm): 16" (40 cm), 40" (100 cm) or longer circular (cir), and set of 4 or 5 double-pointed (dpn).

Size U.S. 7 (4.5 mm): 16" (40 cm) cir and set of 4 or 5 dpn.

Size G-6 (4 mm) crochet hook.

Adjust needle and hook sizes if necessary to obtain the correct gauge.

Notions
Stitch markers (m); cable needle (cn); tapestry needle; waste yarn.

Gauge
20½ sts and 28 rows = 4" (10 cm) in chart A with larger needles, blocked.

Knitting Knowledge

The body of this project is worked flat, and the sleeves are worked in the round. It requires:

- Knitting with circular and double-pointed needles
- Provisional cast-on
- Reading lace and cable charts
- Knitting and purling
- Cable knitting
- Finishing

Notes

The waste yarn you use for holding stitches should be similar in weight to your project yarn and ravel easily without leaving behind bits of fiber, such as a cotton yarn.

When picking up stitches along the top and bottom of the wrap for the border, do so at a ratio of 3:4—pick up 3 stitches, then skip 1 stitch.

STITCH GUIDE

2/2LPC (2 over 2 left purl cross): Sl 2 sts onto cn and hold in front, p2, k2 from cn.
2/2RPC (2 over 2 right purl cross): Sl 2 sts onto cn and hold in back, k2, p2 from cn.

Garter Rib (multiple of 4 sts)
  Rnd 1: Knit.
  Rnd 2: *P2, k2; rep from *.
  Rep Rnds 1 and 2 for patt.

BODY

Cast on
With smaller short cir needle, CO 96 sts using provisional method (Techniques, page 141). Do not join.

NEXT ROW: (WS) Knit.

Change to larger cir needle.

Begin Chart A
Reading RS rows from right to left and WS rows from left to right, work Rows 1–32 one (one, two) time(s), then rep Rows 1–31 (1–31, 1–15) once more.

Piece should measure 9 (9, 11¼)" (23 [23, 28.5] cm) from beg.

Prepare left armhole
NEXT ROW: (WS) Work 15 sts in established patt, join waste yarn and k58, turn, k58, turn, cut waste yarn, leaving a tail; using working yarn again, work in patt to end of row.

Work 95 (111, 127) more rows even until piece measures 22¾ (25, 29½)" (58 [63.5, 75] cm) from beg.

Prepare right armhole
NEXT ROW: (WS) Work 15 sts in established patt, join waste yarn and k58, turn, k58, turn, cut waste yarn, leaving a tail; using working yarn again, work in patt to end of row.

Work 64 (64, 80) more rows even until piece measures 32 (34¼, 41¼)" (81.5 [87, 105] cm) from beg.

Change to smaller long cir needle.

NEXT ROW: (RS) Knit.

BORDER

Remove provisional CO and place 96 sts on smaller short cir needle. With RS facing, place marker (pm), rotate work one-quarter turn with left edge at top, pick up and k166 (178, 190) sts evenly along left (top) edge, pm, rotate work one-quarter turn with CO edge at top, k96, pm, pick up and k166 (178, 190) sts evenly along right (bottom) edge—524 (548, 572) sts. Place marker (pm) for beg of rnd and join for working in rnds, taking care not to twist sts.

INC RND: M1p, [k2 tbl, p2] to 2 sts before next marker, k2 tbl, m1p, slip marker (sm), m1p, [k2 tbl, p2] to next marker, m1, m, m1, [p2, k2 tbl] to 2 sts before next marker, p2, m1, sm, m1, [p2, k2 tbl] to end, m1p—8 sts inc'd.

NEXT RND: P1, [k2 tbl, p2] to 2 sts before marker, k2 tbl, p1, sm, p1, [k2 tbl, p2] to 1 st before marker, k1 tbl, sm, k1 tbl, [p2, k2 tbl] to 2 sts before marker, p2, k1 tbl, sm, k1 tbl, [p2, k2 tbl] to last st, p1.

Cont in established rib patt and inc 1 st before and after each marker on next rnd, then every other rnd, until ribbing measures 2 (2, 2¼)" (5 [5, 5.5] cm). Work inc sts into patt.

BO all sts loosely in patt. Cut yarn, leaving a 6" (15 cm) tail.

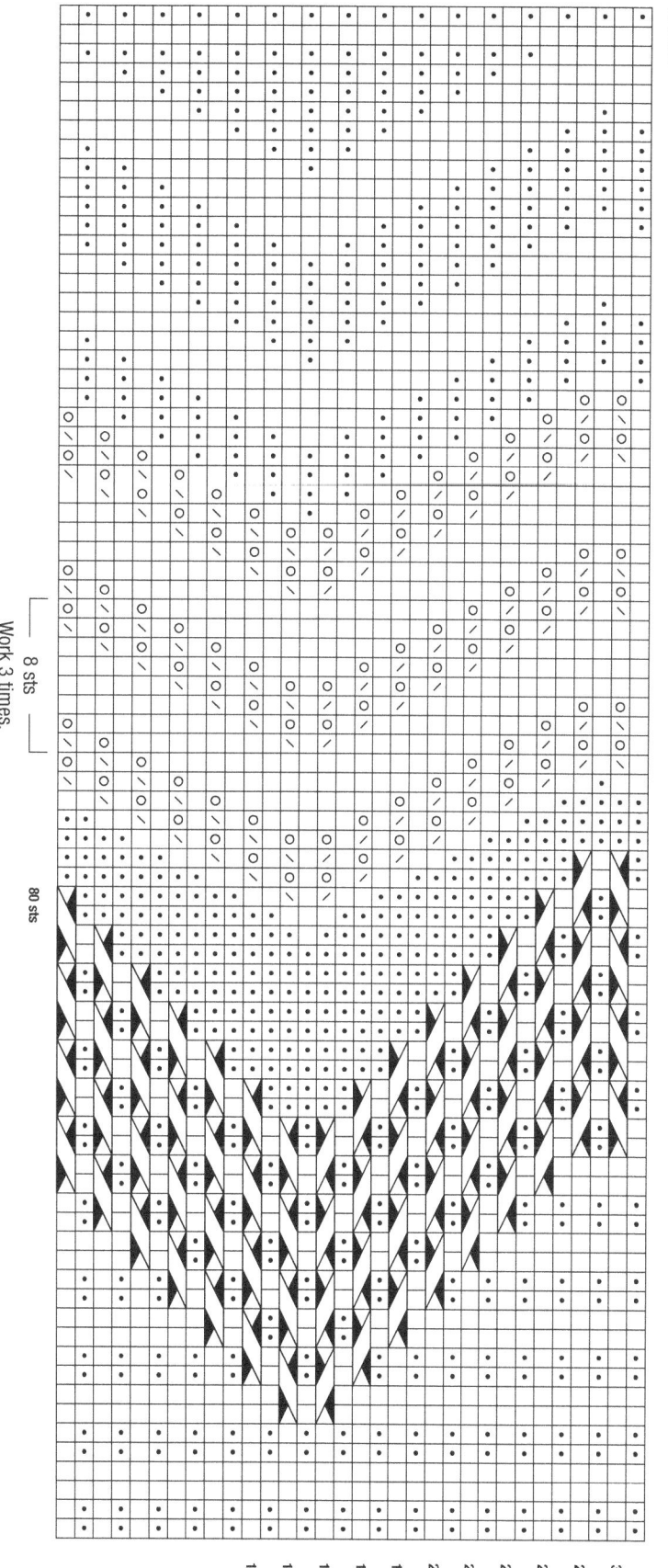

Rosema Wrap

SLEEVES

Remove waste yarn from one armhole and place 116 sts on shorter large cir needle, making sure needle tips are at bottom of armhole. Pm for beg of rnd and join for working in rnds.

Begin Chart B

NEXT RND: K43, pm, work Row 1 of Chart B over next 30 sts, pm, k43.

NEXT RND: K3, [k2, p2] 10 times, sm, work Row 2 of Chart B over next 30 sts, sm, [p2, k2] 10 times, k3.

Keeping first 2 and last 2 sts in St st (knit every rnd), sts outside charted area in garter rib (see Stitch Guide, page 66), work in established patt until sleeve measures 4½ (5½, 5¾)" (11.5 [14, 14.5]), ending with an even-numbered rnd of chart.

Shape sleeve

Change to dpn when there are too few sts to work easily on cir needle.

DEC RND: K2, ssk, work in established patt to last 4 sts, k2tog, k2—2 sts dec'd.

Rep dec rnd every 6 rnds 0 (2, 7) times, every 4 rnds 27 (24, 18) times, then every other rnd 2 (1, 0) time(s)—56 (60, 64) sts rem.

Sleeve should measure 20¾ (21¼, 22¼)" (52.5 [54, 56.5] cm).

Change to smaller dpn.

NEXT RND: Knit.

NEXT RND: *K2 tbl, p2; rep from *.

Rep last rnd until cuff measures 1" (2.5 cm).

BO loosely. Cut yarn, leaving a 6" (15 cm) tail.

FINISHING

Weave in all loose ends, waiting to trim yarn tails until after wrap has been blocked.

Soak finished wrap in cool water with a little wool wash. Lift out and gently squeeze to remove water. Lay it on a towel and roll up to remove excess water. Unroll, shape, and lay out to finished measurements and allow to dry completely.

Chart B

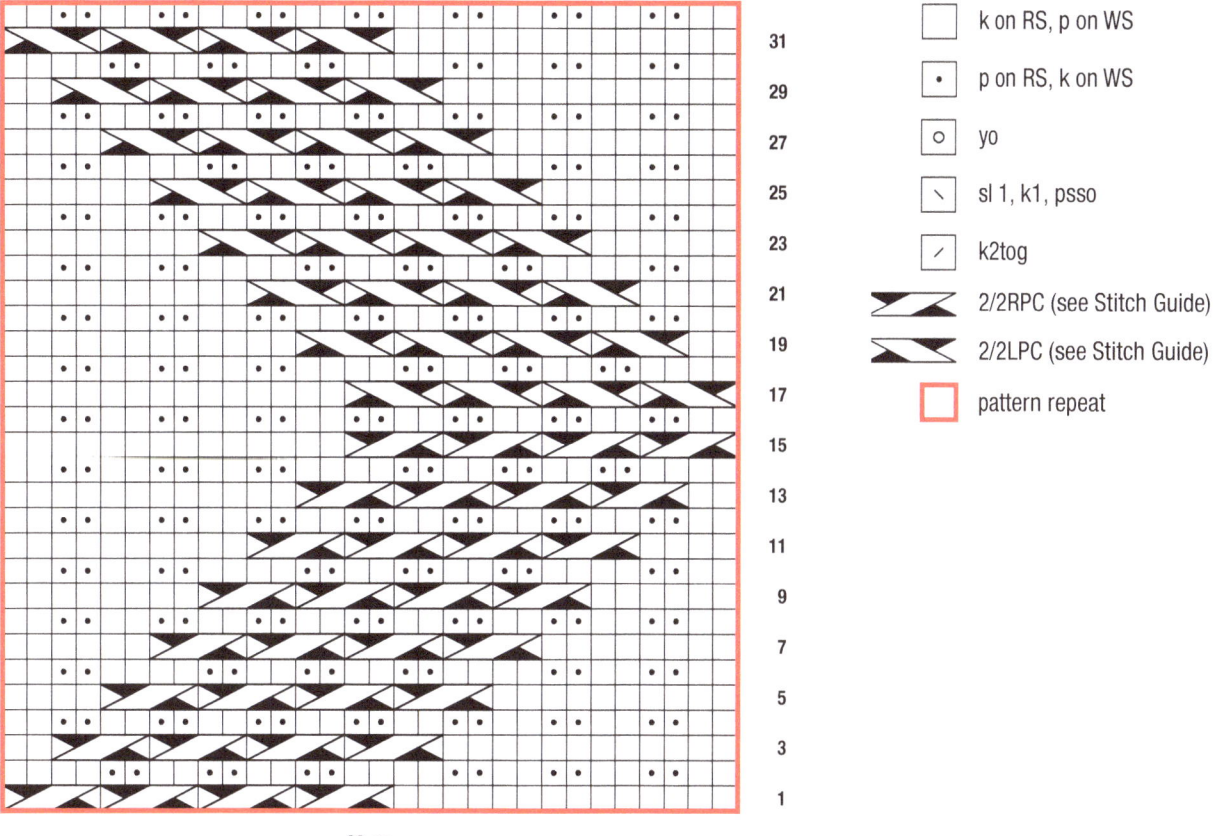

30 sts

	k on RS, p on WS
•	p on RS, k on WS
○	yo
\	sl 1, k1, psso
/	k2tog
	2/2RPC (see Stitch Guide)
	2/2LPC (see Stitch Guide)
	pattern repeat

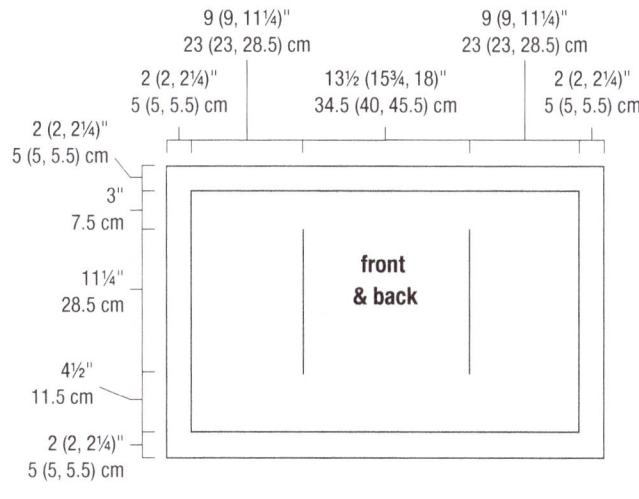

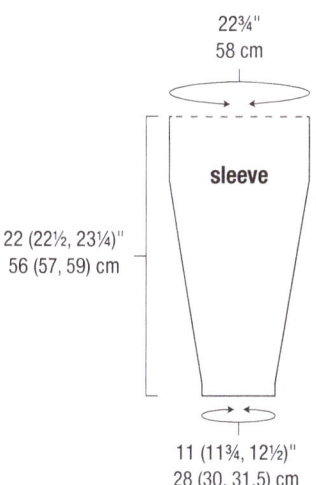

CHAPTER THREE

A Change in Seasons: Wraps & Scarves

In the spring, when heading out before the sun has warmed the air, lightweight scarves and wraps are a pleasing, aesthetic way to add a layer of comfort. Later in the day, the chill of the office or freeze of a movie theater are no match for the coziness of a woolen wrap.

I think of this chapter as the "one-size-fits-most" category because these pieces fit virtually anyone. I love how the scale of these garments allows room for larger, more complex intarsia patterns and lace designs.

APOLLO WRAP

Celebrating the theater facades of the Art Deco era, the Apollo Wrap is designed with bands of intarsia garter stitch. Working from the top down, the texture of garter stitch builds continuity through the piece. Using solid or kettle-dyed yarns will help to highlight the angled sections. The generous size of this wrap also makes it ideal as a lap blanket.

Finished Size
76" x 48" (193 x 122 cm).

Yarn
DK weight (#3 Light).

Shown: Hazel Knits Lively DK (90% superwash merino, 10% nylon; 275 yd [252 m]/130 g): Fudge (A), 4 hanks; Arroyo (B), 3 hanks; Lichen (C), 2 hanks; Frost (D), 1 hank.

Needles
Size U.S. 8 (5 mm): 24" (60 cm), 32" (80 cm), and 60" (150 cm) circular (cir).

Adjust needle size if necessary to obtain the correct gauge.

Notions
Tapestry needle.

Gauge
20 sts and 40 rows = 4" (10 cm) in garter stitch, blocked.

Knitting Knowledge

This project is worked flat and requires:

- Knitting with circular needles
- Casting on and binding off
- Working garter-stitch intarsia
- Finishing

Notes

You will need 3 sources of yarn for yarn A, and two sources of yarn for yarns B, C, and D. Use the schematic (page 75) as a reference while knitting the wrap.

Remember to twist the old yarn over the new one on the wrong side of the work every time you change colors in intarsia. Work the last few stitches of one color and the first few stitches of the new color on the tips of the needles to help create a nice transition. Leave yarn tails of about 6" (15 cm) for weaving in once the piece is completed.

Begin your project with the longest length circular and switch to shorter lengths as needed. This is a fantastic project to consider using an interchangeable set such as skacel by addi™ addiClick set.

STITCH GUIDE

Decrease Bind-off: *K2tog tbl, slip st just worked back to LH needle—1 st dec'd. Rep from * until required number of sts are BO.

WRAP

Section 1
With A, CO 380 sts using the German twisted method (Techniques, page 141).

Work 39 rows in garter st (knit every row), ending with a RS row.

NEXT ROW: (WS) BO 20 sts using dec BO method (see Techniques), knit to end of row—360 sts rem.

Section 2
NEXT ROW: (RS) With A, BO 19 sts, join B and BO 1 more st, cut A, leaving a 6" (15 cm) tail, knit until there are 160 sts on right needle, rejoin A and k20, join second ball of B, knit to end—340 sts rem; 160 sts in each section of B and 20 sts in A.

NEXT ROW: (WS) K160 with B, k20 with A, k160 with B. Make sure to twist yarns when changing colors.

Work 38 more rows as established, ending with a RS row.

NEXT ROW: (WS) With B, BO 20 sts, knit to end of row in established patt—320 sts rem.

Section 3
NEXT ROW: (RS) With B, BO 19 sts, cut B, leaving a 6" (15 cm) tail, join C and BO 1 more st, cut B, leaving a 6" (15 cm) tail, knit until there are 120 sts on right needle, rejoin B and k20, k20 with A, k20 with B, join second ball of C, knit to end—300 sts rem; 140 sts in each section of C, 20 sts in each section of B, and 20 sts in A.

NEXT ROW: (WS) K120 with C, k20 with B, k20 with A, k20 with B, k120 with C. Make sure to twist yarns when changing colors.

Work 38 more rows as established, ending with a RS row.

NEXT ROW: (WS) With C, BO 20 sts, knit to end in patt—280 sts rem.

Section 4

NEXT ROW: (RS) With C, BO 19 sts, cut C, leaving a 6" (15 cm) tail, join A and BO 1 more st, cut C, knit until there are 80 sts on right needle, rejoin C and k20, k20 with B, k20 with A, k20 with B, k20 with C, join a third ball of A, knit to end—260 sts rem; 80 sts at each end in A, 20 sts in A at center, and 20 sts in each section of B and C.

NEXT ROW: (WS) K80 with A, k20 with C, k20 with B, k20 with A, k20 with B, k20 with C, k80 with A. Make sure to twist yarns when changing colors.

Work 38 more rows as established, ending with a RS row.

NEXT ROW: (WS) With A, BO 20 sts, knit to end of row—240 sts rem.

Section 5

NEXT ROW: (RS) With A, BO 19 sts, cut A, leaving a 6" (15 cm) tail, join D and BO 1 more st, knit until there are 40 sts on right needle, rejoin A and k20, k20 with C, k20 with B, k20 with A, k20 with B, k20 with C, k20 with A, join second ball of D, knit to end of row—220 sts rem; 40 sts in each section of D and 20 sts in each section of A, B, and C.

NEXT ROW: (WS) K40 with D, k20 with A, k20 with C, k20 with B, k20 with A, k20 with B, k20 with C, k20 with A, k40 with D. Make sure to twist yarns when changing colors.

Work 38 more rows as established, ending with a RS row.

NEXT ROW: (WS) With D, BO 20 sts, knit to end of row in established patt—200 sts rem.

Section 6

NEXT ROW: (RS) With D, BO 20 sts, knit to end of row in established patt—180 sts rem; 20 sts in each section of A, B, C, and D.

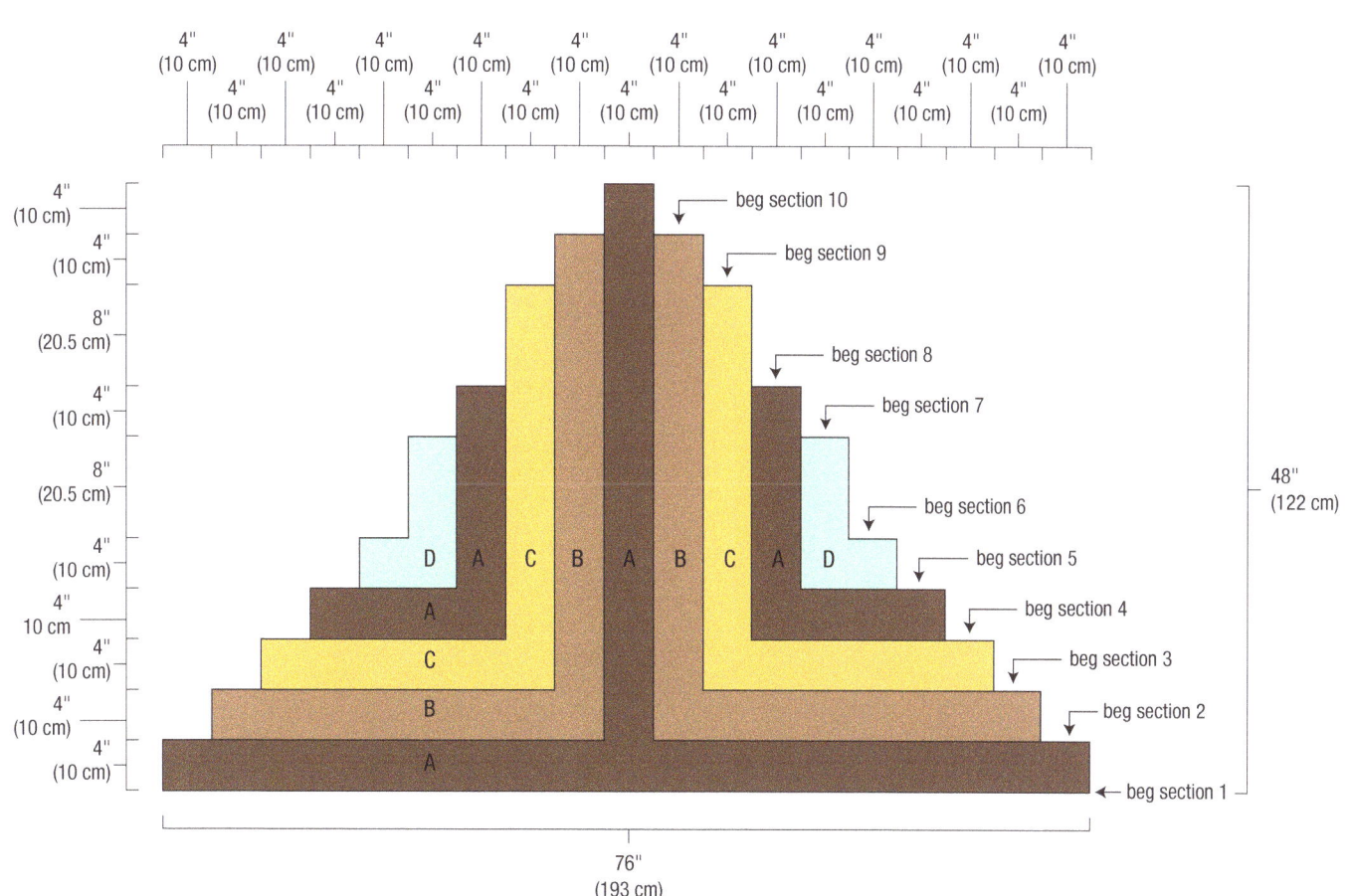

Apollo Wrap

NEXT ROW: (WS) K20 with D, k20 with A, k20 with B, k20 with A, k20 with B, k20 with C, k20 with A, k20 with D. Make sure to twist yarns when changing colors.

Work 78 more rows as established, ending with a RS row.

NEXT ROW: (RS) With D, BO 19 sts, cut D, leaving a 6" (15 cm) tail, and fasten off rem st in D, knit to end of row in established patt—160 sts rem.

Section 7
NEXT ROW: (WS) With D, BO 19 sts, cut D, leaving a 6" (15 cm) tail, and fasten off rem st in D, knit to end of row following color order and established patt—140 sts rem; 20 sts in each section of A, B, and C.

NEXT ROW: (RS) K20 with A, k20 with C, k20 with B, k20 with A, k20 with B, k20 with C, k20 with A. Make sure to twist yarns when changing colors.

Work 38 more rows as established, ending with a RS row.

NEXT ROW: (WS) With A, BO 19 sts, cut A, leaving a 6" (15 cm) tail, and fasten off rem st in A, knit to end of row following color order and established patt—120 sts rem.

Section 8
NEXT ROW: (RS) With A, BO 19 sts, cut A, leaving a 6" (15 cm) tail, and fasten off rem st in A, knit to end of row following color order and established patt—100 sts rem; 20 sts in each section of A, B, and C.

NEXT ROW: (WS) K20 with C, k20 with B, k20 with A, k20 with B, k20 with C. Make sure to twist yarns when changing colors.

Work 78 more rows as established, ending with a RS row.

NEXT ROW: (WS) With C, BO 19 sts, cut C, leaving a 6" (15 cm) tail, and fasten off rem st in C, knit to end of row following color order and established patt—80 sts rem.

Section 9
NEXT ROW: (RS) With C, BO 19 sts, cut C, leaving a 6" (15 cm) tail, and fasten off rem st in C, knit to end of row following color order and established patt—60 sts rem; 20 sts in each section of A and B.

NEXT ROW: (WS) K20 with B, k20 with A, k20 with B. Make sure to twist yarns when changing colors.

Work 38 more rows as established, ending with a RS row.

NEXT ROW: (WS) With B, BO 19 sts, cut B, leaving a 6" (15 cm) tail, and fasten off rem st in B, knit to end of row following color order and established patt—40 sts rem.

Section 10
NEXT ROW: (RS) With B, BO 19 sts, cut B, leaving a 6" (15 cm) tail, and fasten off rem st in B, knit to end of row with A—20 sts rem.

Knit 38 more rows.

Using decrease BO method (see Techniques), BO rem sts. Cut yarn, leaving a 6" (15 cm) tail.

FINISHING

Weave in ends, working tails into their respective color sections. Wait to trim the yarn tails until after the wrap has been blocked.

Soak finished wrap in cool water with a little wool wash. Lift out water and gently squeeze to remove water. Lay it on a towel and roll up to remove excess water. Unroll, shape, and lay wrap flat to dry. Trim yarn tails.

Apollo Wrap 77

D'AMOUR WRAP

The D'Amour Wrap is perfect for the knitter interested in a stranding adventure. The entire wrap is mapped out in a series of detailed charts to navigate the journey. At first glance, the charts appear symmetrical, but upon further exploration you'll see that each side has its own variations, making it unique. Using the technique of locked floats (pages 11–15) makes both the front and back beautiful. Once the stranded portion is complete, an applied I-cord edge finishes the wrap.

Don't let the large charts stop you from tackling this gorgeous piece! Remember what I said earlier about the difference between difficult and time-consuming? Filled with geometric and stylistic designs, this wrap promises to be a showstopper.

Finished Size
53" x 14½" (134.5 x 37 cm).

Yarn
Fingering weight (#1 Super Fine).

Shown: Quince & Co. Finch (100% American wool; 221 yd [202 m]/50 g): #153 Iceland (MC), 5 hanks; #151 Kittywake (CC), 3 hanks.

Needles
Size U.S. 5 (3.75 mm): 36" (90 cm) circular (cir).

Size U.S. 4 (3.5 mm): 36" (90 cm) cir and pair of double-pointed (dpn).

Adjust needle sizes if necessary to obtain the correct gauge.

Notions
Stitch markers (m); waste yarn; tapestry needle.

Gauge
32 sts and 34 rows = 4" (10 cm) in patt using larger needles, blocked.

Knitting Knowledge

This project is worked flat and requires:

- Knitting with circular and double-pointed needles
- Casting on
- Reading charts
- Knitting and purling
- Locking floats
- Working applied I-cord
- Finishing

Notes

This project requires working from several large charts simultaneously. Place markers as specified in cast on to help keep your place.

Remember to keep your yarns in the same order during the entire project. Lock the floating yarn every other stitch.

Learn more about locking floats on pages 11–15.

WRAP

Cast on
With MC, waste yarn, and larger cir needle, CO 419 sts using provisional method (Techniques, page 141). Do not join.

Place markers every 60 stitches to correspond with the way the charts are divided (the last section has 59 sts).

Begin charts
ROW 1: (RS) Beg at right edge of each chart and work Row 1 of all charts in this order: Chart A, place marker (pm), Chart B, pm, Chart C, pm, Chart D, pm, Chart E, pm, Chart F, pm, then Chart G.

ROW 2: (WS) Beg at left edge of each chart and work Row 2 of all charts in this order: Chart G, slip marker (sm), Chart F, sm, Chart E, sm, Chart D, sm, Chart C, sm, Chart B sm, then Chart A.

Work Rows 3–120 as established. Wrap the floating yarn every other stitch on WS of every row.

Cut CC, leaving a 12" (30.5 cm) tail.

NEXT ROW: (RS) With MC only, knit.

Leave these sts on hold on cir needle. Cut yarn, leaving a 12" (30.5 cm) tail.

FINISHING

Note: Beginning the I-cord trim away from the corners of your work allows for a neater finish and helps hide the spot on the edging where it is grafted together. While working, be sure to pick up an entire edge stitch to help minimize holes. See "Working Applied I-Cord" on page 120 for detailed instructions.

Work I-cord edging
Remove provisional CO and place held sts onto smaller cir needle. With MC, beg working applied I-cord along left edge to corner.

To turn corner, work 2 rows of I-cord without joining—(slide sts to right end of dpn, k4) twice—then continue joining I-cord to edge of work as established.

To work along bottom edge, slip 1 held st from provisional CO instead of picking up 1 st.

Turn second corner. Work as for left side until you reach the top, then turn the corner again. Work along the top of the wrap, joining to held sts same as for bottom edge.

Turn the last corner and continue down the left side until ends of I-cord meet. Cut yarn, leaving a 12" (30.5 cm) tail.

Graft ends of I-cord together using the tail threaded in a tapestry needle and Kitchener stitch (see Techniques), taking care not to pull sts tight. Once joined, manipulate the sts until the join resembles neighboring stitches.

Weave in ends, waiting to cut yarn tails until after piece has been blocked. Soak the finished wrap in cool water with a little wool wash. Lift out and gently squeeze to remove water. Lay work on a towel and roll up to remove excess water. Unroll, shape, and lay piece flat to dry.

5 Tips for Knitting from Large Charts

Large charts, such as the one used to knit the D'Amour Wrap and the Savoy Cardigan (page 54), seem intimidating. But when you take them one row at a time, they're much easier to work than they appear. I use these five tips to simplify knitting from charts:

1. Place markers. Just like in lace knitting, stitch markers are your friends. Place them at regular intervals. Take time to count and check your work to make sure that you're staying on track. Remember to mark your chart to correspond with each marker you've placed.

2. Don't panic. Don't remove the needle from your work and start ripping! Rather, take time to count stitches and see if you can locate the error. Usually, it's a dropped stitch, an erroneous decrease, or a sneaky increase. Worst case? You're off a stitch.

In a highly complex pattern, it's probably not going to be noticeable. (Yes, I'm saying don't worry about it!) Identify the section of your work that needs to be remedied and decide how to fix the problem. Sometimes it means tinking back a row or two; other times it means making an improvised correction and then pressing on. In a design that's not rigidly repetitive, it'll be virtually impossible to detect a miscolored stitch.

3. Make copies. I prefer working with paper copies of my charts, although there are electronic programs that allow for chart navigation. Copy each chart and keep them on magnetic boards (I use the ones designed for cross-stitch) and mark each row as it is worked.

4. Unknot the yarn. It's standard for yarns to arrive to the consumer with production knots. Because the spread of each row is considerable in a project such as the D'Amour Wrap, take time to wind all of your yarn into cakes or balls, check for knots, and deal with them accordingly. If the yarn has a high protein-fiber content, then it will most likely spit splice (Techniques, page 141) together. Also, always begin and end yarn at the edge of your work (never in the middle of the row).

5. Slow down. It's not a race. This is probably the most important thing to remember. We know when we start large projects such as this that they will take time to complete. Allow yourself the time needed to craft your work.

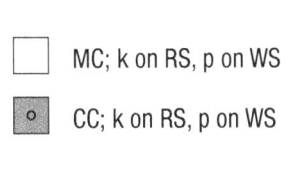

Chart A

 MC; k on RS, p on WS

 CC; k on RS, p on WS

Chart map

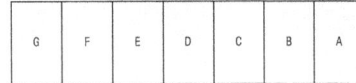

Chart map; Chart A

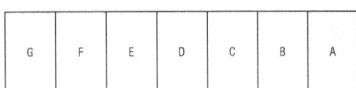

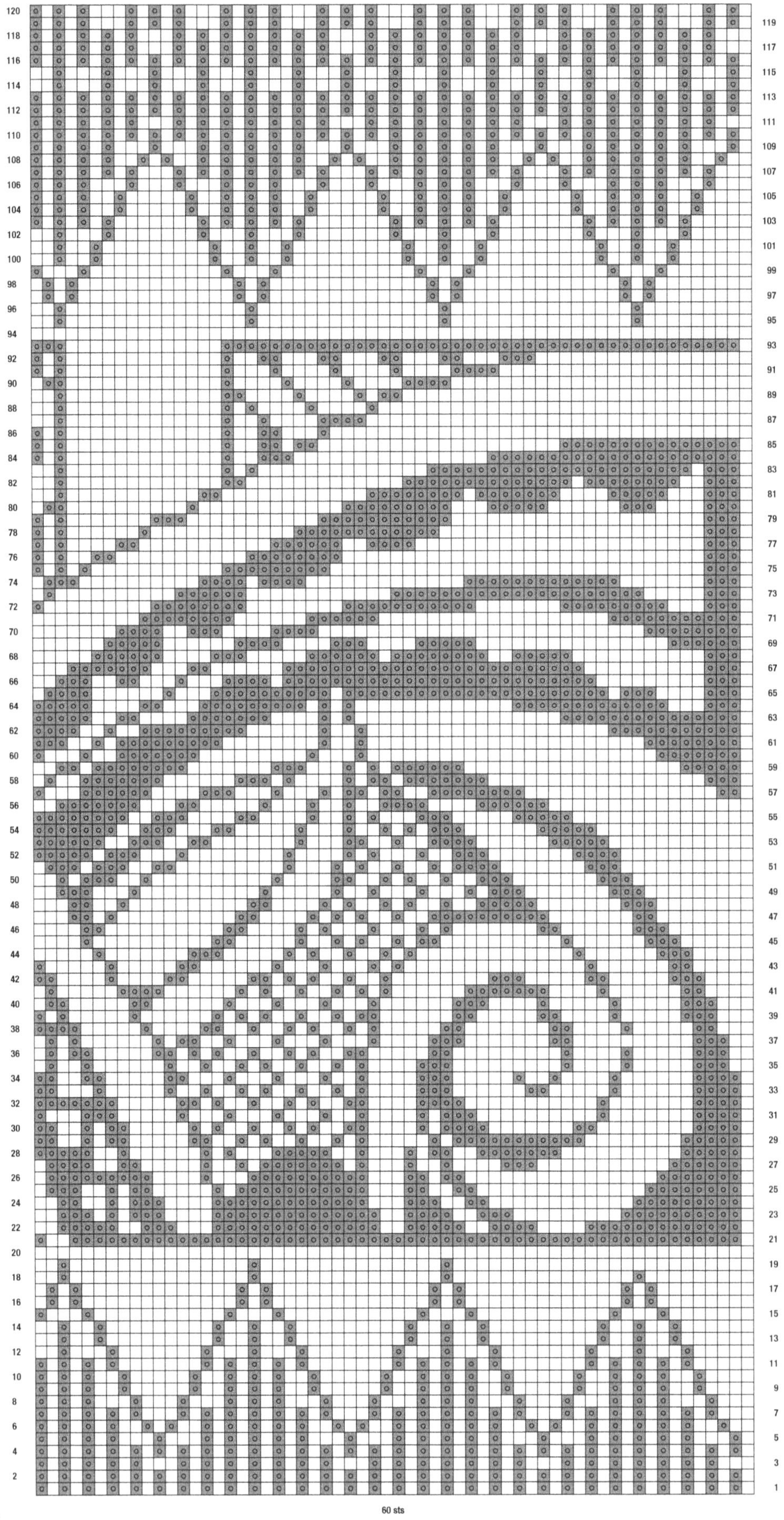

Chart B

Chart map

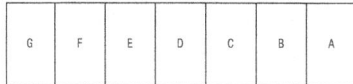

Chart map; Chart B

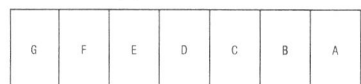

D'Amour Wrap

☐ MC; k on RS, p on WS

○ CC; k on RS, p on WS

Chart map

| G | F | E | D | C | B | A |

Chart map; Chart C

| G | F | E | D | C | B | A |

Chart C

60 sts

84 URBAN KNIT COLLECTION

Chart D

Chart map

G	F	E	D	C	B	A

Chart map; Chart D

G	F	E	D	C	B	A

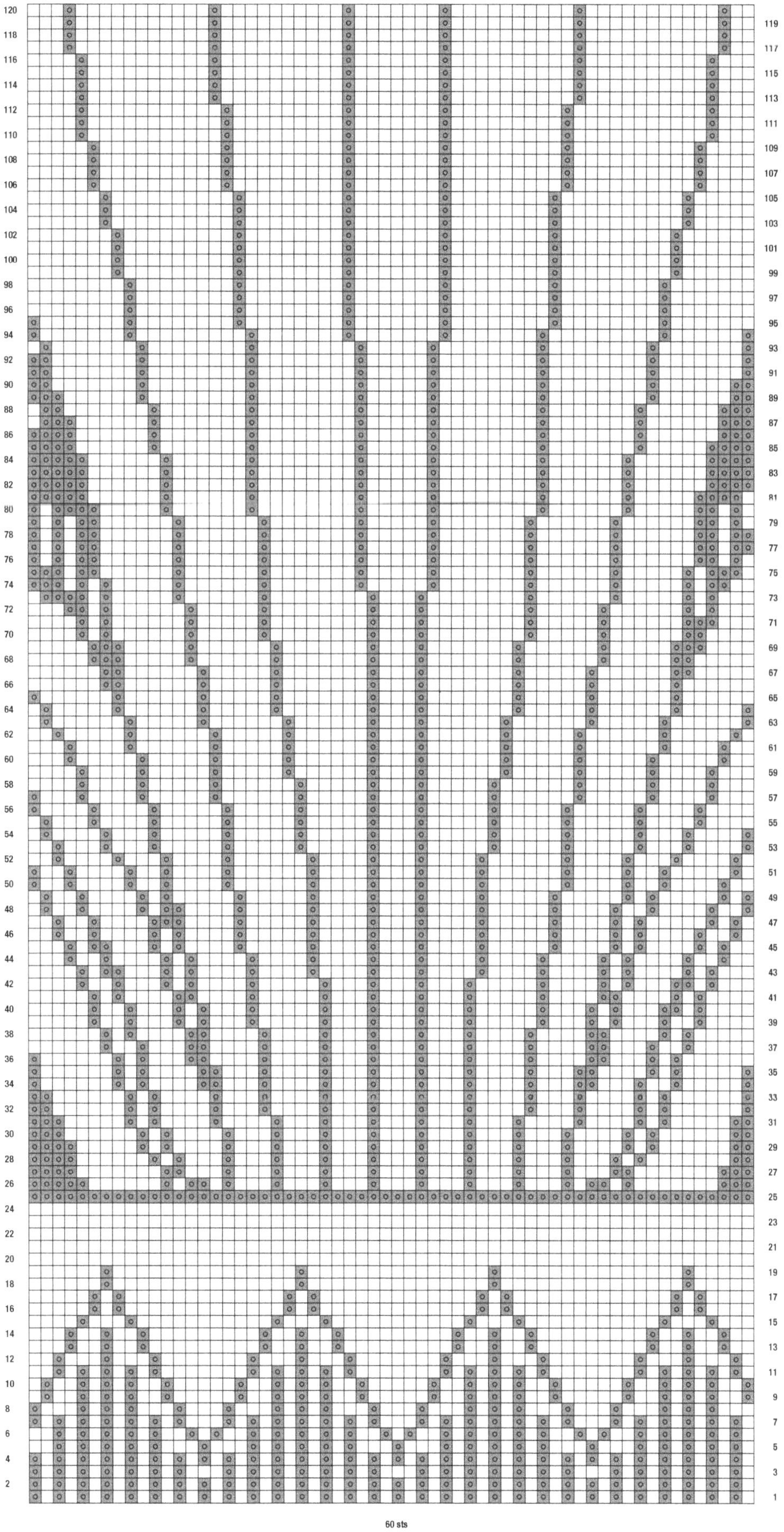

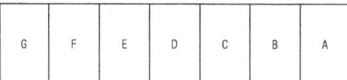

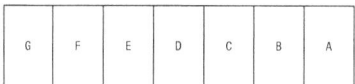

☐ MC; k on RS, p on WS
◉ CC; k on RS, p on WS

Chart map

| G | F | E | D | C | B | A |

Chart map; Chart E

| G | F | E | D | C | B | A |

Chart E

86 URBAN KNIT COLLECTION

Chart F

Chart map

Chart map; Chart F

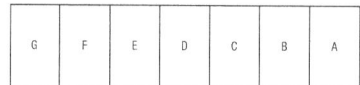

D'Amour Wrap

☐ MC; k on RS, p on WS

◉ CC; k on RS, p on WS

Chart map

G	F	E	D	C	B	A

Chart map; Chart G

G	F	E	D	C	B	A

Chart G

59 sts

D'Amour Wrap

ARCHES SCARF

The stacked, pierced arches of a stone grill seen in the auditorium of an old theater sparked the inspiration for this scarf full of undulating cables. The repeating pattern is mirrored, dancing down the length of this wonderfully wide scarf, which is high enough to protect the back of your neck from a frosty wind.

Finished Size
59¼" x 10" (150.5 x 25.5 cm).

Yarn
Worsted weight (#4 Medium).

Shown: HiKoo Simplinatural (40% baby alpaca, 40% fine merino, 20% mulberry silk; 183 yd [167 m]/100 g): #053 Cabernet, 4 hanks.

Needles
Size U.S. 7 (4.5 mm): 16" (40 cm) circular (cir) or straight.

Size U.S. 8 (5 mm): 16" (40 cm) cir or straight.

Adjust needle sizes if necessary to obtain the correct gauge.

Notions
Stitch markers (m); cable needle (cn); tapestry needle.

Gauge
22½ sts and 25 rows = 4" (10 cm) in chart patt with larger needles, blocked.

Knitting Knowledge

This project is worked flat and requires:

- Knitting with circular needles
- Casting on and binding off
- Reading charts
- Knitting and purling
- Cable knitting
- Finishing

Notes

Most of the cabling on this scarf is worked on RS rows, leaving the WS rows full of knit and purl stitches. Every once in a while, however, the center cable wraps over itself, which requires cabling on a WS row. Pay careful attention to this cable and remember that it is worked differently than the others.

To keep from stretching cabled stitches, choose a cable needle with a diameter equal to or smaller than the project needle size, or consider working the cables without a cable needle.

STITCH GUIDE

1x1 Ribbed Cast-On: Make a slipknot, leaving a yarn tail that is 6" (15 cm) long. Insert needle into loop, then snug it up. This first stitch looks like a purl stitch.

Insert RH needle tip as if to knit, yarn over and pull through a loop, then place the new stitch on LH needle tip.

*Insert RH needle tip as if to purl between 2 sts on LH needle tip, yarn over and pull loop through a loop, then place the new stitch on LH needle tip (*figures 1 and 2*). Insert RH needle tip as if to knit between first 2 sts on LH needle tip, yarn over and pull through a loop, then place the new stitch on LH needle tip. Repeat from * until the required number of stitches are on LH needle tip; the final stitch is the last loop made.

Seed Stitch Bind-Off: Use a needle one or two sizes smaller than for the project for the bind-off.

P1, move yarn to back, sl st just made to LH needle tip, k2tog–1 st BO (*figure 3*).

*Move yarn to front, sl st from RH needle tip to LH needle tip, p2tog–1 st BO (*figure 4*). Move yarn to back, sl st from RH needle tip to LH needle tip, k2tog–1 st BO; repeat from * until all sts have been BO.

2/1LPC (2 over 1 left purl cross): Sl 2 sts onto cn and hold in front, p1, k2 from cn.

2/1RPC (2 over 1 right purl cross): Sl 1 st onto cn and hold in back, k2, p1 from cn.

2/2LC WS (2 over 2 left cross on wrong side): Sl 2 sts onto cn and hold in front, p2, p2 from cn.

2/2LPC (2 over 2 left purl cross): Sl 2 sts onto cn and hold in front, p2, k2 from cn.

2/2RPC (2 over 2 right purl cross): Sl 2 sts onto cn and hold in back, k2, p2 from cn.

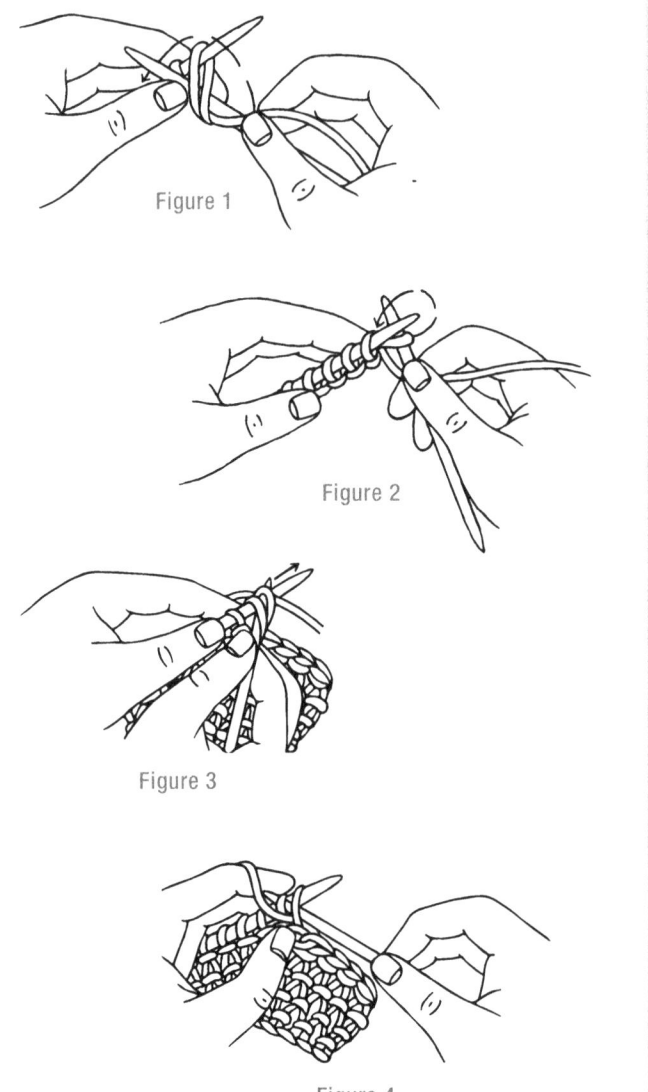

Figure 1

Figure 2

Figure 3

Figure 4

SCARF

Cast on

With smaller needles, CO 56 sts using the 1x1 Ribbed Cast-On method (see Stitch Guide).

ROW 1: (RS) *K1, p1; rep from *.

ROW 2: (WS) *P1, k1; rep from *.

Work 3 more rows in established patt.

Change to larger needles.

SET-UP ROW: (WS) [P1, k1] twice, place marker (pm), [p1, k1] 3 times, p5, [k1, p1] 5 times, k1, p5, [k1, p1] 5 times, k1, p5, [k1, p1] twice, k1, pm, [p1, k1] twice.

Begin chart

Work Rows 1–24 of the chart 14 times, slipping markers as you come to them.

Work Rows 1–23 once more. Piece should measure 58¼" (148 cm) from beg.

- ☐ k on RS, p on WS
- • p on RS, k on WS
- 2/1LPC (see Stitch Guide)
- 2/1RPC (see Stitch Guide)
- 2/2LPC (see Stitch Guide)
- 2/2RPC (see Stitch Guide)
- 2/2LC WS (see Stitch Guide)
- ☐ pattern repeat

Chart A

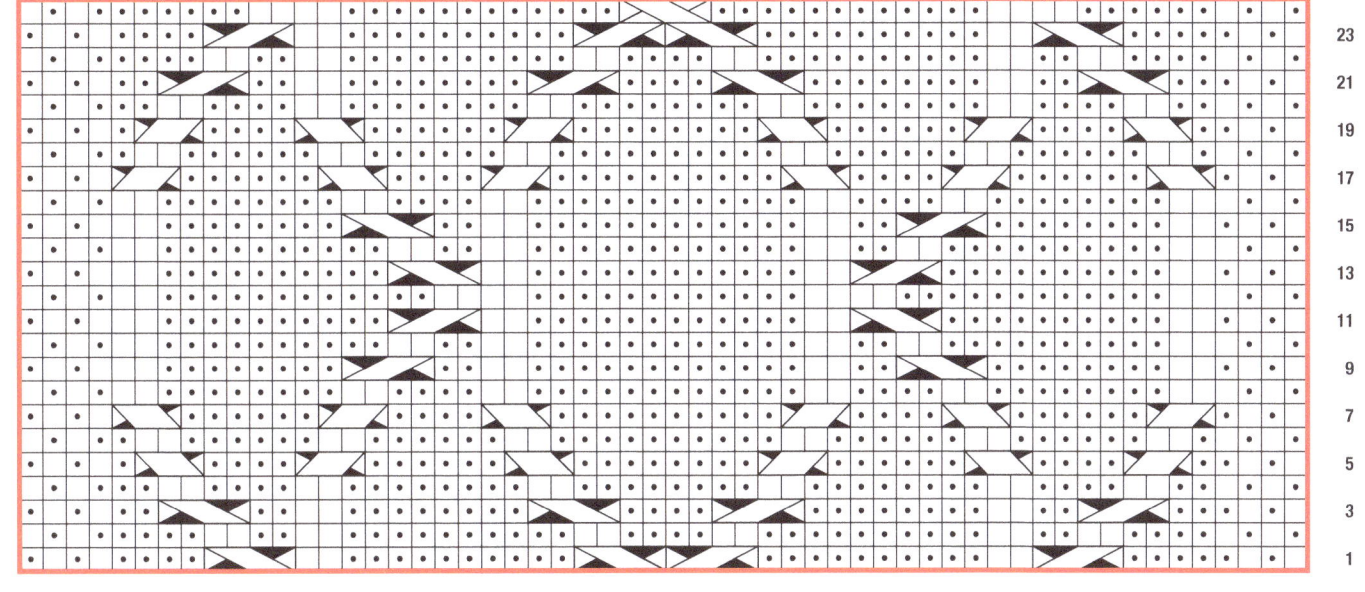

56 sts

NEXT ROW: (WS) (P1, k1) twice, remove marker, (p1, k1) 3 times, p5, (k1, p1) 5 times, k1, p5, (k1, p1) 5 times, k1, p5, (k1, p1) twice, k1, remove marker, (p1, k1) twice.

Change to smaller needles.

NEXT ROW: (RS) *K1, p1; rep from *.

NEXT ROW: (WS) *P1, k1; rep from *.

Work 3 more rows in established patt.

BO using seed st method (see Stitch Guide). Cut yarn, leaving a 6" (15 cm) tail.

FINISHING

Weave in all ends, waiting to cut yarn tails until after piece has been blocked.

Soak piece in cool water with a little wool wash. Lift out and gently squeeze to remove water. Lay on a towel and roll up to remove excess water. Unroll, shape, and lay piece flat to dry.

SUNBURST SHAWL

Beads radiate from the center of this half-circle shawl, adding texture and sparkle. Want the pattern to make a bolder statement? Try using beads in a contrasting color. The result is a shawl with beautiful drape and a satisfying weight. Take your time with the beading process, and be sure to pick up extra—some won't slide easily onto your hook. Don't let the beading intimidate you; it's more manageable than it looks, and the finished piece is worth every moment.

Finished Size
65" x 36" (165 x 91.5 cm).

Yarn
Sportweight (#2 Fine).

Shown: Malabrigo Yarn Arroyo (100% superwash merino; 335 yd [306 m]/100 g): Reflecting Pool, 5 hanks.

Needles
Size U.S. 8 (5 mm): 36" (90 cm) circular (cir).

U.S. size 11 (0.8 mm) steel crochet hook.

Adjust needle and hook sizes if necessary to obtain the correct gauge.

Notions
Stitch markers (m); tapestry needle.

260 grams of size 6/0 seed beads (shown: about 4,400 Toho silver-lined teal).

Gauge
18 sts and 26 rows = 4" (10 cm) in pattern, blocked.

Knitting Knowledge
This project is worked flat and requires:

- Knitting with circular needles
- Casting on and binding off
- Reading charts
- Working with beads
- Knitting and purling
- Increasing and decreasing
- Finishing

Adding Beads
To place beads, work to stitch requiring a bead. Place a bead on the tip of the crochet hook. Lift the next stitch on the LH needle using the hook, and then slide the bead over this stitch. Replace the stitch on the LH needle and work as normal. Refer to Techniques, page 141, for more information.

GARTER TAB

Cast on

CO 3 sts using the German twisted method (Techniques, page 141).

Knit 6 rows. Do not turn.

Rotate work 90 degrees clockwise. Pick up and knit 3 sts along side of tab. Rotate work clockwise again. Pick up and knit 3 sts along CO edge—9 sts.

SHAWL

SET-UP ROW 1: RS K2, (k1f&b) 4 times, k3—13 sts.

SET-UP ROW 2: WS K3, purl to last 3 sts, k3.

SET-UP ROW 3: RS Knit.

SET-UP ROW 4: WS K3, purl to last 3 sts, k3.

SET-UP ROW 5: (RS) K3, place marker (pm), m1r, *k1, m1l, pm, k1, pm, m1r; rep from * 2 more times, k1, m1l, pm, k3—21 sts.

SET-UP ROW 6: (WS) K3, purl to last 3 sts, k3.

SET-UP ROW 7: (RS) Knit.

SET-UP ROW 8: (WS) K3, purl to last 3 sts, k3.

SET-UP ROW 9: (RS) K3, slip marker (sm), m1r, *knit to m, m1l, sm, k1, sm, m1r; rep from * to last 3 sts, m1l, sm, k3—8 sts inc'd.

Rep Rows 6–9 two more times, then rep Rows 6–8 once more—45 sts.

Begin chart

Note: The charts represents the 3 stitches within each section, but it does not include the knit stitches at the beginning and end of the work or the knit stitch that separates each repeat.

NEXT ROW: (RS) K3, [sm, work Row 1 of Chart A to m and place beads as indicated, sm, k1] 3 times, sm, work Row 1 of Chart A to last m, sm, k3—8 sts inc'd.

Keeping first and last 3 sts in garter st (knit every row) and the st between each repeat in St st (knit RS rows, purl WS rows), work Rows 2–100 of Chart A, then Rows 1–71 of Chart B—389 sts.

EDGING

Work 3 rows in St st.

Work 4 rows of garter st.

BO all sts loosely. Cut yarn, leaving a 6" (15 cm) tail.

FINISHING

Weave in ends, waiting to cut yarn tails until after piece has been blocked.

Soak finished shawl in a bath of cool water with a little wool wash. Lift out of bath and gently squeeze to remove excess water. Lay the shawl on a towel and roll up to remove excess water. Unroll, shape, and lay flat to dry.

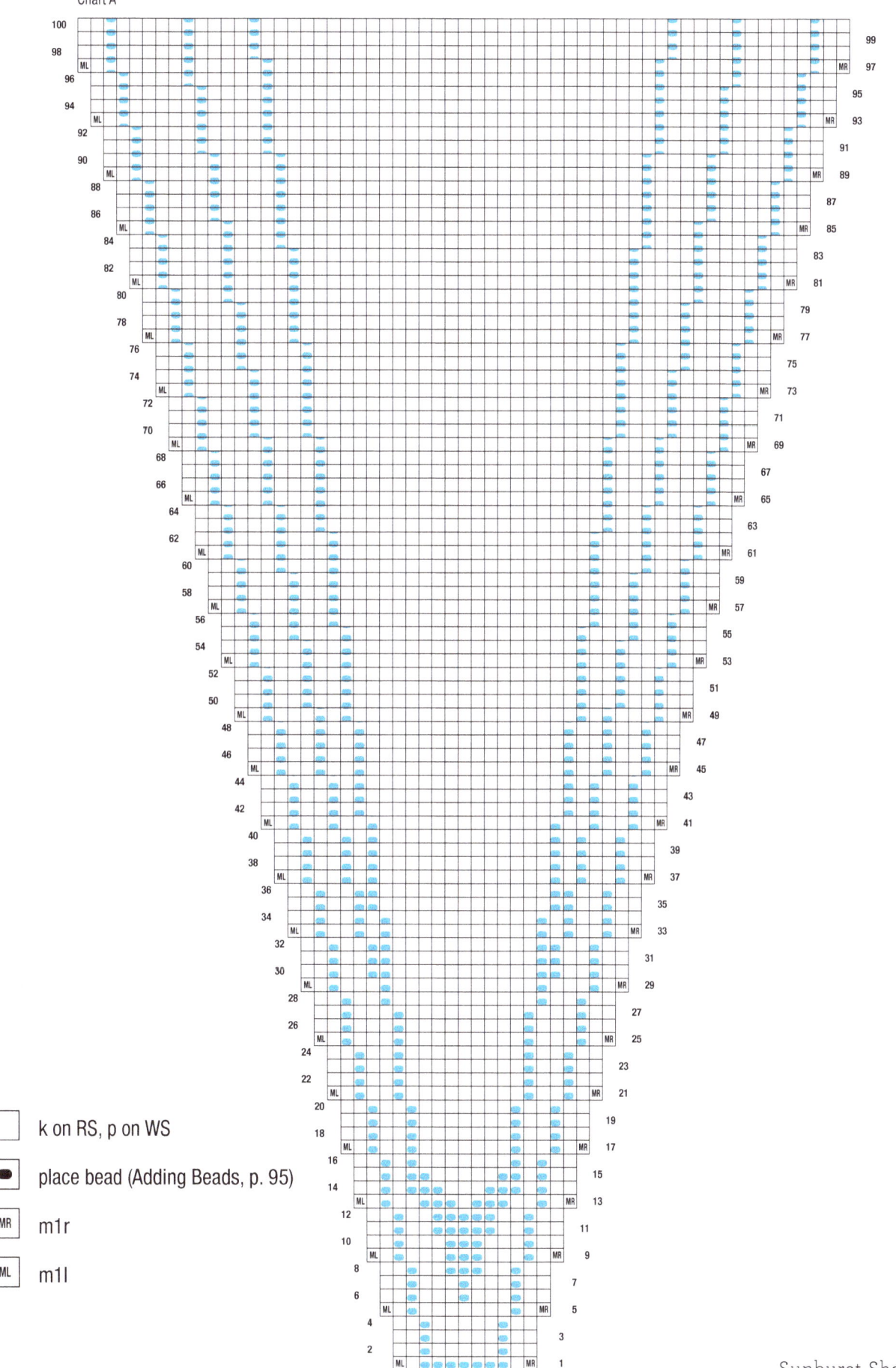

Sunburst Shawl 97

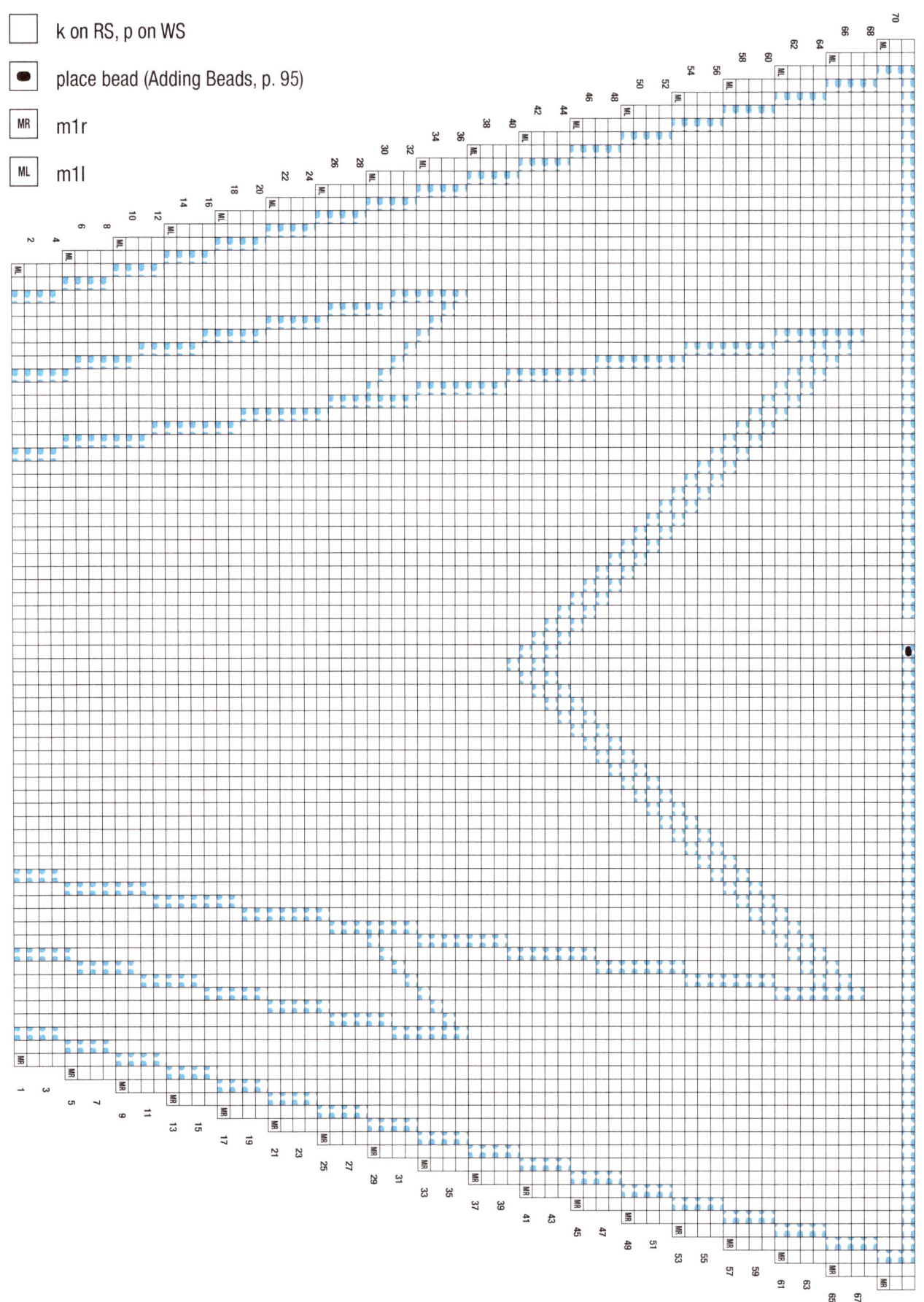

98 URBAN KNIT COLLECTION

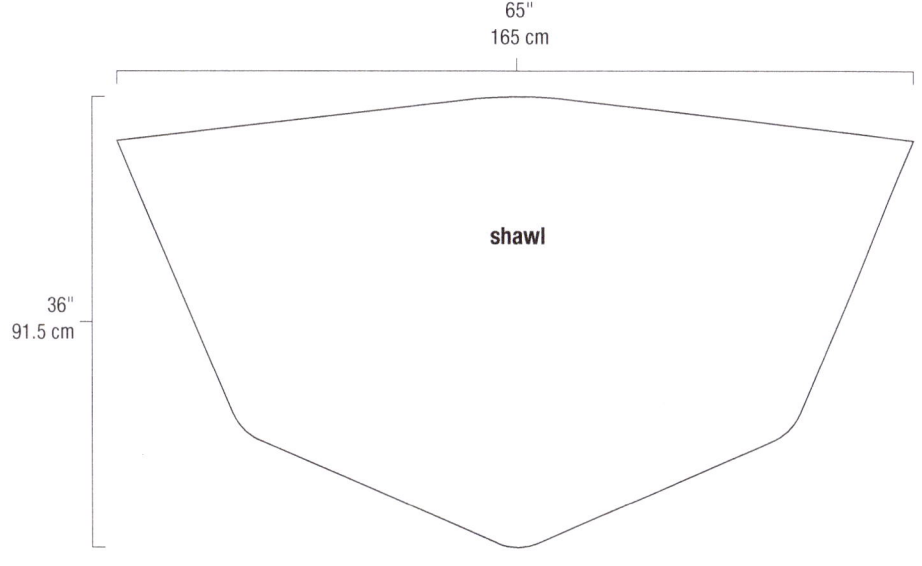

Sunburst Shawl

ZEPHYR SCARF

Surrounded by a seed-stitch border, the pattern in this scarf found its inspiration in the wrought-iron doors of a public school in Romania. The Greek key pattern lends itself to this type of repetitive pattern. Even after it was transformed into fabric, it reminds me of the iron gates guarding doorways throughout downtown San Francisco.

Finished Size
7¼" x 76" (18.5 x 193 cm).

Yarn
Sportweight (#2 Fine).

Shown: Shibui Knits Staccato (70% superwash merino, 30% silk; 191 yd [175 m]/50 g): #2003 Ash (MC), 3 skeins; #2032 Field (CC), 2 hanks.

Needles
Size U.S. 4 (3.5 mm): 16" (40 cm) circular (cir) or straight.

Adjust needle size if necessary to obtain the correct gauge.

Notions
Stitch markers (m); tapestry needle.

Gauge
37½ sts and 31½ rows = 4" (10 cm) in chart patt, blocked.

Knitting Knowledge

This project is worked flat and requires:
- Knitting with circular needles
- Casting on and binding off
- Reading charts
- Knitting and purling
- Working stranded knitting and intarsia
- Locking floats

Notes

This is an opportunity to really show off how lovely locked floats (page 11–15) make the back of the fabric. Take advantage of this technique, and you'll end up with a scarf that looks great on both sides.

To keep the thickness of the fabric consistent throughout the charted portions, begin weaving the CC on the first stitch of the first chart and continue weaving the unused color along the back throughout the center field of the scarf.

In the center of the pattern (where the design flips), you'll find two plain rows worked in MC with no patterning. I recommend carrying the CC behind these stitches, using the locked float technique, so that the thickness of the fabric is consistent through the piece.

SCARF

Cast on
With MC, CO 68 sts using the German twisted method (Techniques, page 141).

ROW 1: (RS) *K1, p1; rep from *.

ROW 2: (WS) *P1, k1; rep from *.

Rep these 2 rows 3 more times.

Work Chart A
NEXT ROW: (RS) Work 4 sts in seed st as established, place marker (pm), join CC, and work Row 1 of Chart A over 60 sts, pm, work to end in seed st as established.

Keeping the first and last 4 sts in seed st and, slipping markers as you come to them, work Rows 2–22 of Chart A. Remember to wrap and lock the CC when starting each row of colorwork.

Work Chart B
NEXT ROW: (RS) Work 4 sts in seed st as established, slip marker (sm), work Row 1 of Chart B over 60 sts, sm, work to end in seed st as established.

Cont in established patt, work Rows 2–18 of Chart B, then rep chart Rows 1–18 thirteen more times.

Work Chart C
NEXT ROW: (RS) Work 4 sts in seed st as established, sm, work Row 1 of Chart C (page 104) over 60 sts, sm, work to end in seed st as established.

Cont in established patt, work Rows 2–36 of Chart C for center of scarf.

Work Chart D
Note: This chart is the flipped version of Chart B.

NEXT ROW: (RS) Work 4 sts in seed st as established, sm, work Row 1 of Chart D (page 106) over 60 sts, sm, work to end in seed st as established.

Cont in established patt, work Rows 2–18 of Chart B, then rep chart Rows 1–18 thirteen more times.

Work Chart E
NEXT ROW: (RS) Work 4 sts in seed st as established, sm, work Row 1 of Chart E (page 106) over 60 sts, sm, work to end in seed st as established.

Cont in established patt, work Rows 2–22 of Chart E.

Cut CC, leaving a 6" (15 cm) tail.

Work 8 rows in seed st. BO all sts using the decrease bind-off method (see page 74). Cut yarn, leaving a 6" (15 cm) tail.

FINISHING

Weave in ends.

Soak the scarf in cool water with a little wool wash, shape, and pin flat to dry.

- MC; k on RS, p on WS
- CC; k on RS, p on WS
- pattern repeat

Chart A

60 sts

Chart B

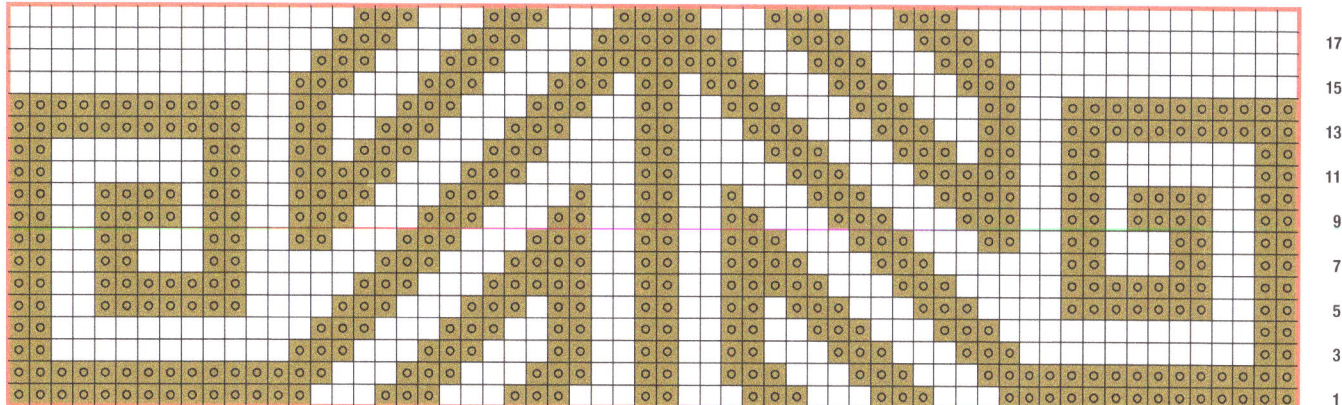

60 sts

Zephyr Scarf 103

☐ MC; k on RS, p on WS

◦ CC; k on RS, p on WS

Chart C

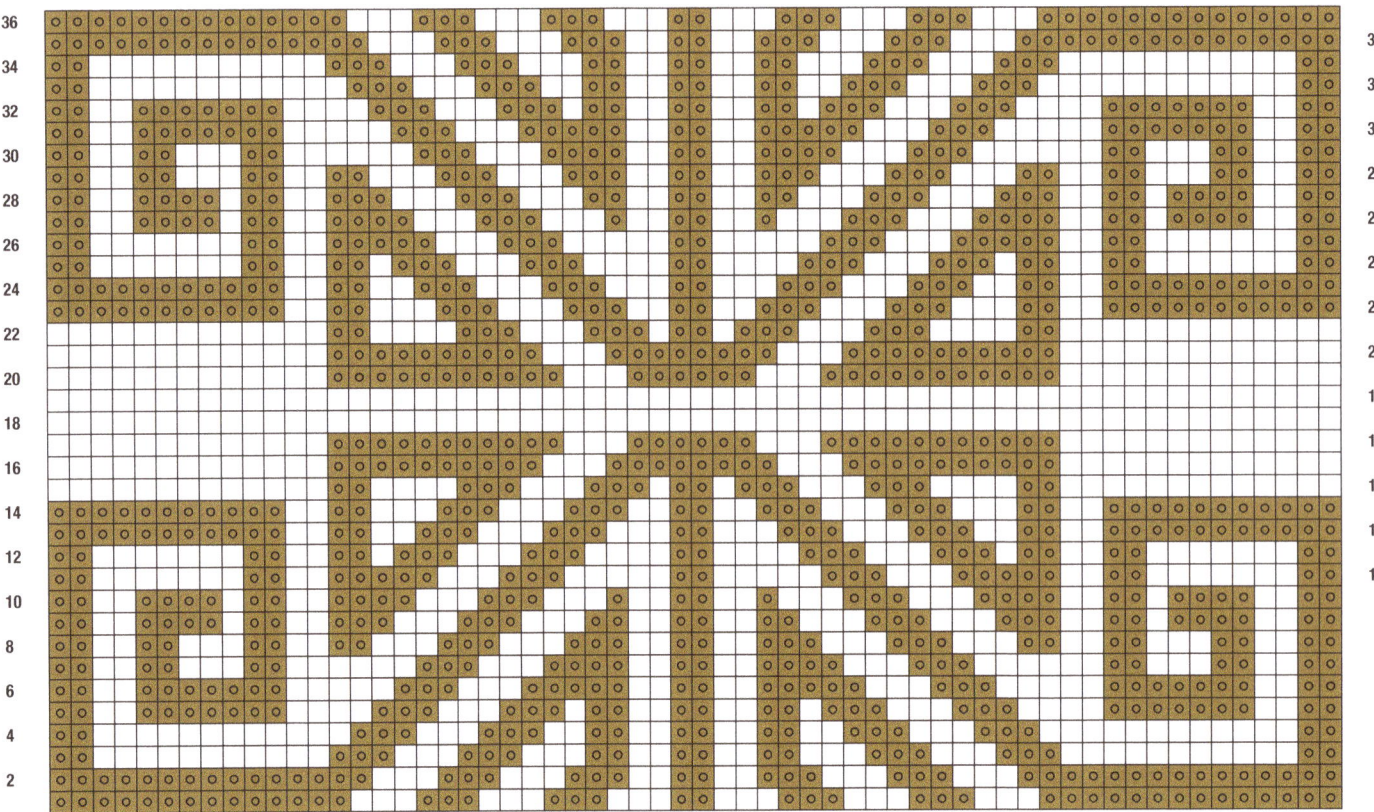

60 sts

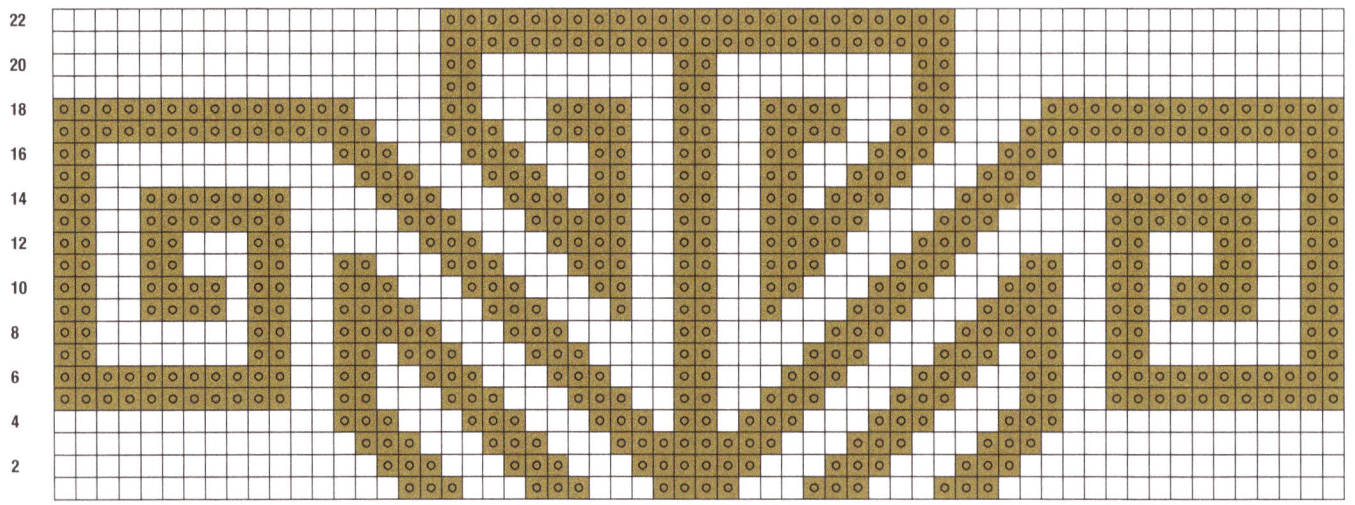

CHAPTER FOUR

Souvenir Shopping: Accessories

As a person who is always looking for a little reminder of my journeys, I turn to two different collections: yarn and rocks. (Yes, you read that right!) When I travel, I often find a small rock on the ground and use a permanent marker to inscribe the date and location. This rock collection lives in a lidded glass jar in my studio and reminds me of so many adventures.

Similarly, when I'm traveling, a trip to a yarn shop (or two) is certainly on the agenda. Yarn is a great souvenir! Started on a trip, small souvenir projects are a memorable way to practice new techniques, and they beg to be taken to the coffee shop, on vacation, or to the local knit night.

TOWN-SQUARE HATS

I see colorwork motifs everywhere I go—from the scrolls in ironwork—to the cascades of water in a town-square fountain. This pattern pays homage to the careful planning that was involved in the creation of town squares, full of icons, public buildings, and landmarks. The two-color ribbed brim of the first hat holds a repeated vertical fountain motif. Beneath this colorful brim lives a band of stretchy, single-color ribbing. The alternate chart provides a more geometric option.

The yarn I selected for this project has so much yardage that I created another chart for a second hat. Both samples were worked using the same two skeins of yarn.

While working the charts, it's helpful to lock the floating yarn every other stitch. Keeping the yarns in the same order will help keep consistent color dominance and also make the inside of the project almost as lovely as the outside.

Finished Size
20" (51 cm) circumference and 7½" (19 cm) tall with brim folded.

Yarn
Fingering weight (#1 Super Fine).

Shown: Blue Moon Fiber Arts Socks That Rock lightweight (100% superwash merino; 405 yd [370 m]/146 g). One hank each of 2 colors.

Hat A: Buttah (MC) and Antiquated System (CC).

Hat B: Antiquated System (MC) and Buttah (CC).

Needles
Size U.S. 1 (2.25 mm): 16" (40 cm) circular (cir).
Size U.S. 2 (2.75 mm): 16" (40 cm) cir and set of 5 double-pointed (dpn).
Adjust needle sizes if necessary to obtain the correct gauge.

Notions
Stitch marker (m); tapestry needle.

Gauge
36 sts and 37 rnds = 4" (10 cm) in chart patt with larger needles, blocked.

Knitting Knowledge

This project is worked in the round and requires:
- Knitting with circular and double-pointed needles
- Casting on
- Reading charts
- Knitting and purling
- Two-color ribbing
- Turned hems
- Wrap & turn
- Locking floats
- Decreasing
- Finishing

Notes

While working on double-pointed needles, be sure to keep the stitch tension even between needles.

BRIM

Cast on

With larger cir needle and MC, CO 180 sts using the German twisted method (Techniques, page 141).

Place marker (pm) for beg of rnd and join for working in rnds, being careful not to twist sts. Join CC.

NEXT RND: *K1 with CC, p1 with MC; rep from *, making sure to bring MC to back after each purl st.

Rep last rnd until piece measures 1½" (3.8 cm) from CO. Cut CC, leaving a 6" (15 cm) tail.

NEXT RND: Knit.

TURNING RND: Purl.

NEXT RND: Sl 1, remove m, move sl st back to LH needle, w&t, p1, k1, pm for new beg of rnd, *p1, k1; rep from *, remembering to pick up wrap and work it with the st it wraps.

Change to smaller cir needle. Cont in established rib until piece measures 1¼" (3.2 cm) from turning rnd. Change to larger cir needle.

NEXT RND: Knit.

CROWN

Begin chart

NEXT RND: Reading chart from right to left, *work Row 1 of either chart (depending on the hat you're making) over 36 sts; rep from * around.

Work Rnds 2–58 as established, changing to dpn when there are too few sts rem to work comfortably on cir needle—10 sts rem.

Cut yarns, leaving 6" (15 cm) tails.

FINISHING

Using a tapestry needle, thread each tail through rem sts twice, gently pull to close hole and fasten off securely on WS. Weave in all ends.

Wait to trim yarn tails until after the piece has been blocked.

Soak hat in cool water with a little wool wash. Lift out and gently squeeze to remove water. Lay piece on towel and roll up to remove excess water. Unroll, shape, and lay flat to dry.

Chart A

Chart B

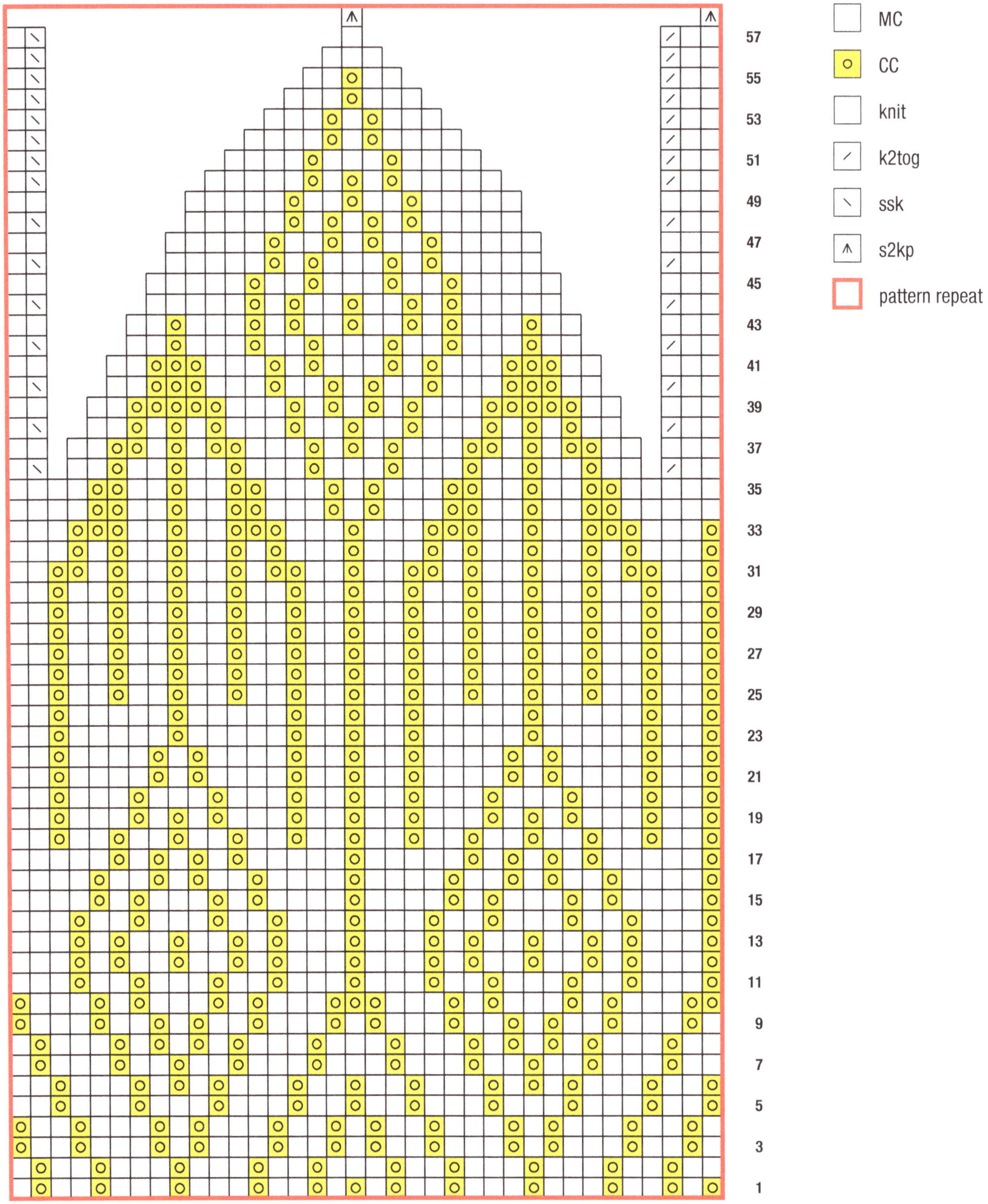
57
55
53
51
49
47
45
43
41
39
37
35
33
31
29
27
25
23
21
19
17
15
13
11
9
7
5
3
1
MC
CC
knit
k2tog
ssk
s2kp
pattern repeat

Town Square Hats 115

RITZ COWL

This colorwork cowl showcases a bold repeating oval motif connected by seed beads. I am particularly enamored with the way the seed beads sparkle but aren't noticed right away. They add a touch of magic to this cowl, while the applied I-cord adds structure and stability. Want a bolder look? Consider using a bead in a color complementary to your contrasting-color yarn.

Because beads are added on only a few rounds and in locations clearly indicated by the chart, this is a good project for those just learning how to use beads in their knitting.

Finished Size
24¾ (40¾)" (63 [103.5] cm) circumference and 11" (28 cm) wide.

Shown in size 40¾" (103.5 cm).

Yarn
Sportweight (#2 Fine).

Shown: Blue Sky Alpacas Sport Weight (100% baby alpaca; 110 yd [100 m]/50 g): #512 Eggplant (MC), 3 (5) hanks; #507 Light Gray (CC), 2 (4) skeins.

Needles
Size U.S. 4 (3.5 mm): double-pointed (dpn).

Size U.S. 5 (3.75 mm): 24" (60 cm) circular (cir).

U.S. size 11 (0.8 mm) steel crochet hook.

U.S. size E-4 (3.5 mm) crochet hook.

Adjust needle and hook sizes if necessary to obtain the correct gauge.

Notions
Stitch marker (m); tapestry needle; waste yarn.

36 (72) grams of size 6/0 seed beads (shown: 624 [1,032] Toho higher-metallic teal green iris)

Gauge
29½ sts and 27 rnds = 4" (10 cm) over chart patt with larger needles, blocked.

Knitting Knowledge
This project is worked in the round and requires:
- Knitting with circular and double-pointed needles
- Casting on
- Reading charts
- Knitting and purling
- Increasing and decreasing
- Managing floats
- Knitting with beads
- Working applied I-cord
- Finishing

Notes
When beads are placed, they sit on the stitch below (see "Adding Beads," page 95). The symbols on the chart indicate where to place the beads. The first row is worked before joining in the round to offer a bit more knitting, which will help you avoid twisting the cast-on stitches.

Some rounds beginning with CC include a slipped stitch to create a less obvious end of round. Slip the first stitch only, then continue working the stitches as normal for the balance of the round. On rounds where only one color is used, continue to carry and lock the floating yarn in back of every other stitch. Doing this will help maintain an even thickness in your fabric.

COWL

Cast on

With larger needle, waste yarn, and MC, CO 182 (301) sts using the provisional method (Techniques, page 141). Do not join.

Knit 1 row. Do not turn. Place marker (pm) for beg of rnd and join for working in rnds, being careful not to twist sts.

Begin chart

RND 1: Join CC. Work 7-st rep of Row 1 of the chart (page 120) 26 (43) times around.

Work Rnds 2–17, rep Rnds 1–17 three more times, then work Rnds 18–20 once.

NEXT RND: Cut CC, leaving a 6" (15 cm) tail.

FINISHING

Work applied I-cord (page 120).

With MC and dpn, CO 4 sts using the provisional method.

*Slide sts to right tip of needle. Bring yarn across back of dpn, k3, sl 1 pwise, yo, knit first st on cowl, pass slipped st and yo over st just knit—4 sts rem on dpn.

Rep from * until all cowl sts have been worked. Cut yarn, leaving 12" (30.5 cm) tail.

Use Kitchener st (see Techniques) to join ends of applied I-cord.

Remove provisional CO from other edge of cowl and place sts on cir needle. Work applied I-cord edging along edge same as first edge.

Weave in all ends, waiting to trim yarn tails until after piece has been blocked.

Soak in cool water with a little wool wash. Lift out of bath and gently squeeze to remove water. Lay piece on towel and roll up to remove excess water. Unroll, shape, and lay flat to dry. Trim ends.

- ☐ MC
- ☐ CC
- ● place bead (Adding Beads, p. 95)
- V sl 1 wyb at beg of rnd only, knit with MC in every rem rep around
- ☐ pattern repeat

Work once.
17-row rep Work 4 times.
7 sts

Working Applied I-Cord

With MC, waste yarn, and dpn, CO 4 sts using the provisional method (Techniques, page 141).

*Slide sts to right end of dpn. Bring yarn across back of dpn, k3 sts, sl 1 pwise, yo, insert right needle tip into next st on edge, pick up and k1, pass yo and sl st over last st and off needle—4 sts rem.

Rep from *, until ends of I-cord meet. Cut yarn, leaving a 12" (30.5 cm) tail. Use tail threaded in tapestry needle and Kitchener st (see Techniques) to join ends of I-cord.

Weave in all ends, following that color's path in the work.

ELLINGTON MITTENS

Stranded colorwork creates a wonderfully insulating fabric because it traps air between the yarns. The small loop-and-button closure keeps these mittens together when not in use. It also provides a lovely opportunity to use a unique vintage button!

Finished Size
6½" (16.5 cm) hand circumference and 9¼" (23.5 cm) tall.

To make a larger or smaller mitten, knit with larger or smaller needles.

Yarn
Fingering weight (#1 Super Fine).

Shown: Classic Elite Yarns Alpaca Sox (60% alpaca, 20% merino, 20% nylon; 450 yd [411.5 m]/100 g): #1816 Oatmeal (MC), #1807 Viridis (CC1), and #1879 Indigo Patina (CC2), 1 skein each.

Needles
Size U.S. 2 (2.75 mm): set of 5 double-pointed (dpn).

Size C-2 (2.75 mm) crochet hook.

Adjust needle and hook sizes if necessary to obtain the correct gauge.

Notions
Stitch markers (m); tapestry needle; waste yarn.

One ½" (13 mm) button.

Gauge
36 sts and 35 rnds = 4" (10 cm) in chart patt, blocked.

Knitting Knowledge

This project is started in the flat, then is continued in the round. It requires:

- Knitting with circular and double-pointed needles
- Casting on
- Reading charts
- Knitting and purling
- Increasing and decreasing
- Finishing

Note

The pattern for this mitten is the same for both hands. There will be plenty of leftover yarn for a second pair.

CUFF

Cast on

With MC, CO 58 sts using the German twisted method (Techniques, page 141). Do not join.

NEXT ROW: (RS) *K1 with MC, join k1 with CC2; rep from * to end. Do not turn.

Note: Be sure to hold yarns in the same order throughout the entire project.

Distribute sts evenly over 4 dpn. Place marker (pm) for beg of rnd and join for work in rnds, being careful not to twist sts.

Begin Chart A

Reading all chart rows from right to left, work Rows 1–18 of Chart A in K1, P1 two-color rib (see Techniques); cuff should measure 2" (5 cm) from CO.

Change to St st (knit every rnd), change colors as indicated on chart, and cont as follows:

THUMB GUSSET

INC RND 1: Work Row 19 of Chart A to end, pm, work Row 1 of Chart B (page 127)—59 sts.

INC RND 2: Work Row 20 of Chart A to m, slip marker (sm), work Row 2 of Chart B—2 sts inc'd.

Work Rows 21–43 of Chart A and Rows 3–25 of Chart B—84 sts; 58 sts for hand and 26 sts for thumb.

Place last 26 sts on waste yarn for thumb, then join to work in rnds—58 sts rem.

HAND

Work Rows 44–82 of Chart A—14 sts rem.

Divide sts evenly with first 7 sts on one dpn and rem 7 sts on second dpn.

Cut yarns, leaving 6" (15 cm) tails. Graft rem sts tog using Kitchener st (see Techniques).

THUMB

Place held 26 thumb sts back on 3 dpn. Rejoin MC and CC2.

Begin Chart B

NEXT RND: In gap at top of opening, pick up and k1 with MC, and pick up and k1 with CC2, then work Row 26 of Chart B to end—28 sts.

Pm for beg of rnd and join for working in rnds. Work Rows 27–40 of chart as established.

Cut CC1, leaving 6" (15 cm) tail. Cont with MC only.

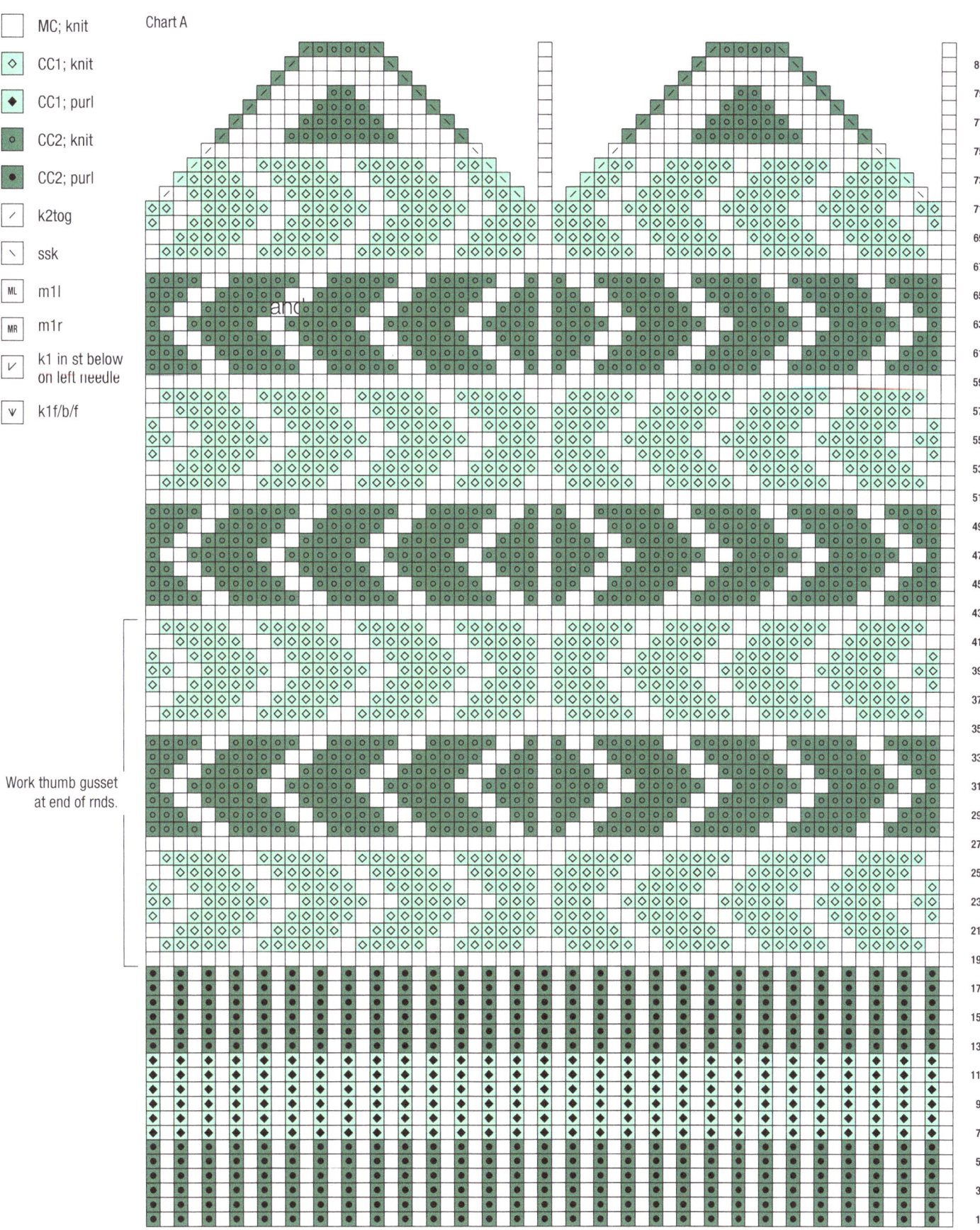

Ellington Mittens

Shape top

RND 1: (K4, k2tog) 4 times, k4—24 sts rem.

RND 2: (K3, k2tog) 4 times, k4—20 sts rem.

RND 3: (K2, k2tog) 5 times—15 sts rem.

RND 4: (K1, k2tog) 5 times—10 sts rem.

RND 5: (K2tog) around—5 sts rem.

Cut yarn, leaving a 6" (15 cm) tail. Thread tail through rem sts twice, pull tight to close hole, and fasten off on WS.

FINISHING

With crochet hook and MC, work a small chain loop (figure 1) of 3–5 sts on the thumb edge of one cuff, securing both ends to create button loop. Sew small button to cuff of other mitten in same location.

Cut yarn, leaving a 6" (15 cm) tail.

Weave in all loose ends, waiting to cut yarn tails until after the pieces have been blocked.

Soak mittens in cool water with a little wool wash. Lift out and gently squeeze to remove water. Lay them on a towel and roll up to remove excess water. Unroll, shape, and lay flat to dry.

Figure 1

Chart B

28 sts

Symbol	Meaning
☐	MC; knit
◇	CC1; knit
◆	CC1; purl
○	CC2; knit
●	CC2; purl
/	k2tog
\	ssk
ML	m1l
MR	m1r
⌄	k1 in st below on left needle
ⱴ	k1f/b/f

DORIAN COWL

The Dorian cowl honors urban public transit maps by interpreting them as a series of traveling stitches and cables. Gently spun wool yarn adds to Dorian's insulating properties, and the large chart keeps the project interesting. Of course, the provisional cast-on takes a little extra time, but I believe the I-cord edging is quite worth the effort. But what do I love most about cowls? They are perfect for keeping the neck warm, and there's no chance they might get caught in a car door or fly away with a brisk breeze.

Finished Size
23 (46)" (58.5 [117] cm) circumference and 9½" (24 cm) wide.
Cowl shown measures 23" (58.5 cm).

Yarn
Aran weight (#4 Medium).

Shown: Manos del Uruguay Wool Clasica (100% wool; 138 yd [126 m]/100 g): #29 Steel, 2 (3) skeins.

Needles
Size U.S. 10 (6 mm): circular (cir).

Size U.S. 9 (5.5 mm): double-pointed (dpn).

U.S. size G-6 (4 mm) crochet hook.

Adjust needle sizes if necessary to obtain the correct gauge.

Notions
Stitch markers (m); cable needle (cn); tapestry needle; waste yarn.

Gauge
19½ sts and 23½ rnds = 4" (10 cm) in chart patt with larger needles, blocked.

Knitting Knowledge
This project is worked in the round and requires:
- Knitting with circular and double-pointed needles
- Casting on
- Reading charts
- Knitting and purling
- Working with a cable needle
- I-cord bind-off
- Finishing

Note
The first row is worked before joining in the round to help avoid twisting the work.

STITCH GUIDE

2/1LPC (2 over 1 left purl cross): Sl 2 sts onto cn and hold in front, p1, k2 from cn.

2/1RC (2 over 1 right cross): Sl 1 st onto cn and hold in back, k2, k1 from cn.

2/1RPC (2 over 1 right purl cross): Sl 1 st onto cn and hold in back, k2, p1 from cn.

COWL

Cast on
With larger needle, working yarn, and waste yarn, CO 112 (224) sts using the provisional method (Techniques, page 141). Do not join.

Purl 1 row. Do not turn. Place marker (pm) for beg of rnd and join for working in rnds, being careful not to twist sts.

Begin chart
Note: Although most of the cables indicate the stitch worked off the cable needle should be purled, a few require that stitch to be knitted.

RND 1: Work 56-st rep of Row 1 of the chart 2 (4) times around.

As you work around the cowl, you'll find that some of the cables necessary to complete the motif overlap at the end and beginning of the round. In these instances, move the marker indicating the beginning of the round, but be aware that the location of the end of the round does not change.

Work Rnds 2–47 of chart.

Purl 2 rnds.

FINISHING

Work applied I-cord (page 120).

With dpn, working yarn, and waste yarn, CO 4 sts using the provisional method.

*Slide sts to right tip of needle. Bring yarn across back of dpn, k3, sl 1 pwise, yo, slip first st of cowl, pass first slipped st and yo st just slipped—4 sts rem on dpn.

Rep from * until all cowl sts have been worked.

Cut yarn, leaving a 6" (15 cm) tail.

Use Kitchener st (see Techniques) to join ends of I-cord.

Remove provisional CO from other edge of cowl and place sts on cir needle. Join yarn.

Purl 2 rnds.

Rep I-cord edging same as first edge.

Weave in all ends, waiting to trim yarn tails until after the piece has been blocked.

Soak in cool water with a little wool wash. Lift piece out of bath and gently squeeze to remove water. Lay it on a towel and roll up to remove excess water. Unroll, shape, and lay flat to dry. Trim ends.

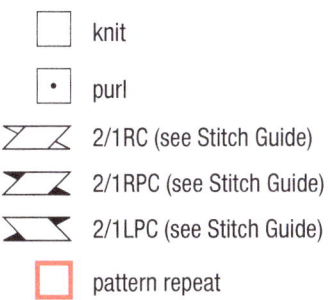

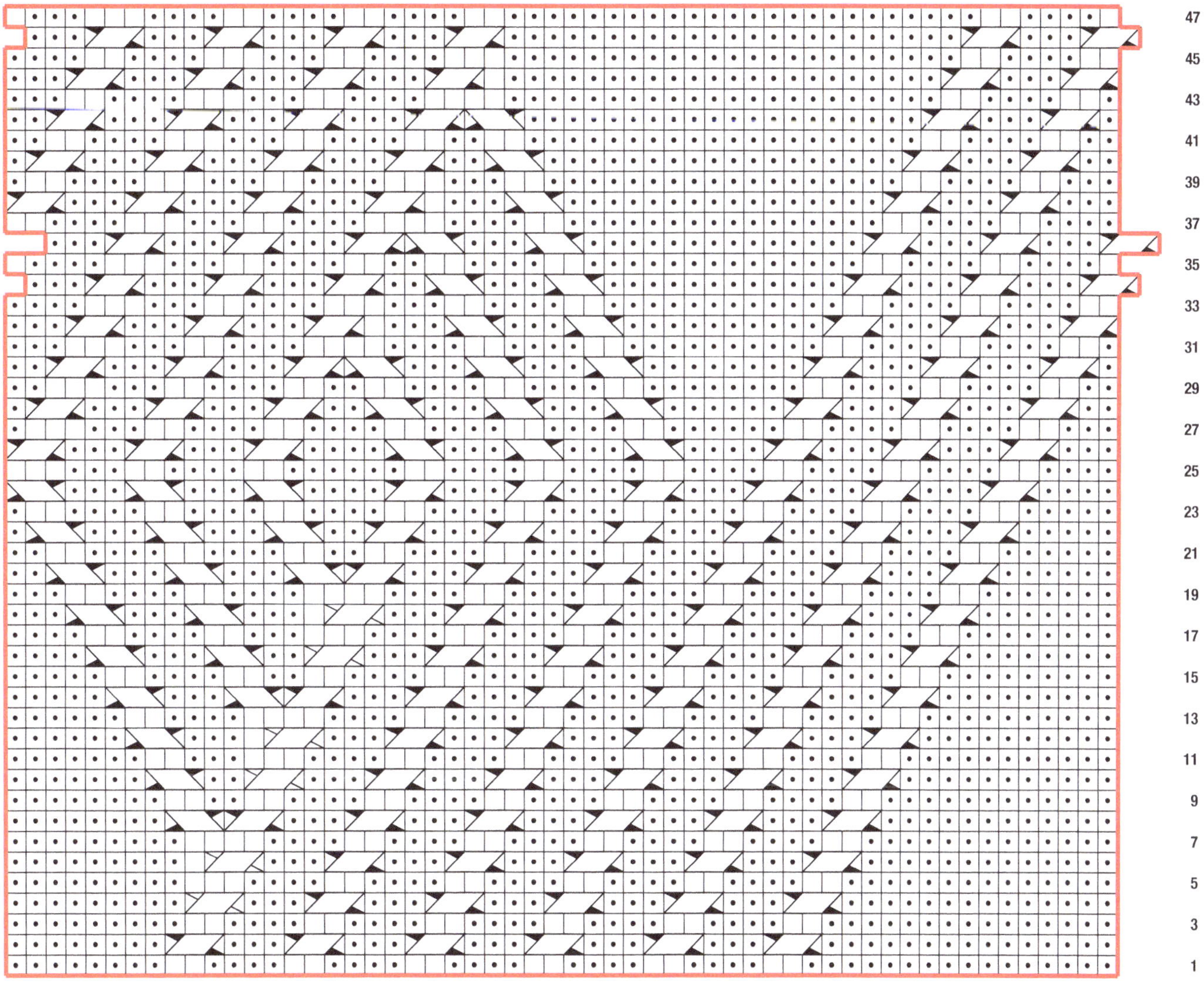

Notes: End rnds 33 and 45 one st before end of rnd and use the last st as first st of cable as follows:
sl 1 to cn and hold in back, remove beg-of-rnd m, k1, replace beg-of-rnd m, k1, then p1 from cn.

End rnd 35 two sts before end of rnd and use the last 2 sts as first sts of cable as follows:
sl 1 to cn and hold in back, sl 1, remove beg-of-rnd m, sl 1 back to left needle, k2, replace beg-of-rnd m, p1.

Dorian Cowl

SKYSCRAPER HAT

One of my most vivid childhood memories is from when my dad brought me and my sisters to the roof of a skyscraper he was building in Louisville, Kentucky. Preparing us for the photo, he had me stand on the rooftop ledge and backed up with the camera to get us all in the frame. As he snapped that photo with the entire world behind us, I felt as though I was going to plummet to my demise there and then—but I didn't!

Worked in the round, this hat features twisted traveling stitches and carefully concealed decreases that mirror and honor the thoughtful engineering that goes into skyscraper construction. Using the German twisted cast-on at the beginning of the hat allows for a touch more stretch at the brim.

Finished Size
22¼" (56.5 cm) circumference and 7¼" (18.5 cm) tall.

Yarn
Worsted weight (#4 Medium).

Shown: Brooklyn Tweed Shelter (100% Targhee-Columbia wool; 140 yd [128 m]/50 g).

For Hat A: #18 Button Jar, 1 hank.

For Hat B: #12 Meteorite, 1 hank (page 155).

For Hat C: #21 Hayloft, 1 hank (page 155).

For Hat D: #22 Artifact, 1 hank (page 155).

Needles
Size U.S. 4 (3.5 mm): 16" (40 cm) circular (cir) and set of 5 double-pointed (dpn).

Adjust needle sizes if necessary to obtain the correct gauge.

Notions
Stitch marker (m); cable needle (cn); tapestry needle.

Gauge
23 sts and 29 rnds = 4" (10 cm) in chart patt, blocked.

Knitting Knowledge

This project is worked in the round and requires:

- Working with circular and double-pointed needles
- Casting on
- Reading charts
- Knitting and purling
- Working twisted stitches
- Cable knitting
- Finishing

Notes

While working on dpn when shaping the top of the hat, be sure to keep the stitch tension even between needles.

To add optional height to the hat, work 2x2 ribbing for 1½" (3.8 cm). Knit 1 round, and then begin chart.

This optional ribbed brim is not pictured in the samples.

STITCH GUIDE

Twisted Stitches: Insert needle into the back of the stitch. Wrap yarn as usual. Pull yarn through stitch.

1/1LC (1 over 1 left cross): Sl 1 st onto cn and hold in front, k1, k1 tbl from cn.

1/1LPC (1 over 1 left purl cross): Sl 1 st onto cn and hold in front, p1, k1 tbl from cn.

1/1RC (1 over 1 right cross): Sl 1 st onto cn and hold in back, k1 tbl, k1 from cn.

1/1RPC (1 over 1 right purl cross): Sl 1 st onto cn and hold in back, k1 tbl, p1 from cn.

BRIM

Cast on

With cir needle, CO 128 sts using the German twisted method (Techniques, page 141).

Place marker (pm) for beg of rnd and join for working in rnds, being careful not to twist sts.

BODY & CROWN

Begin chart

RND 1: Working Row 1 of the chart, work 32-st rep 4 times around.

Work Rnds 2–53 of chart as established, changing to dpn when there are too few sts rem to work comfortably on cir needle—8 sts rem.

Note: Rounds starting with a s2kp begin with the last stitch from the previous round. When beginning the new round, place the last stitch of the previous round onto the left-hand needle and treat it as the first stitch for this round. Place a marker after working the first decrease to indicate the beginning of the round.

FINISHING

Cut yarn, leaving a 6" (15 cm) tail.

Using a tapestry needle, thread tail through rem sts twice, gently pull to close hole and fasten off securely on WS. Weave in all ends, waiting to trim yarn tails until after piece has been blocked.

Soak hat in cool water with a little wool wash. Lift out hat and gently squeeze to remove water. Lay piece on a towel and roll up to remove excess water. Unroll, shape, and let dry.

knit

purl

k1 tbl

s2kp

m1p

1/1RC (see Stitch Guide)

1/1LC (see Stitch Guide)

1/1RPC (see Stitch Guide)

1/1LPC (see Stitch Guide)

no stitch

pattern repeat

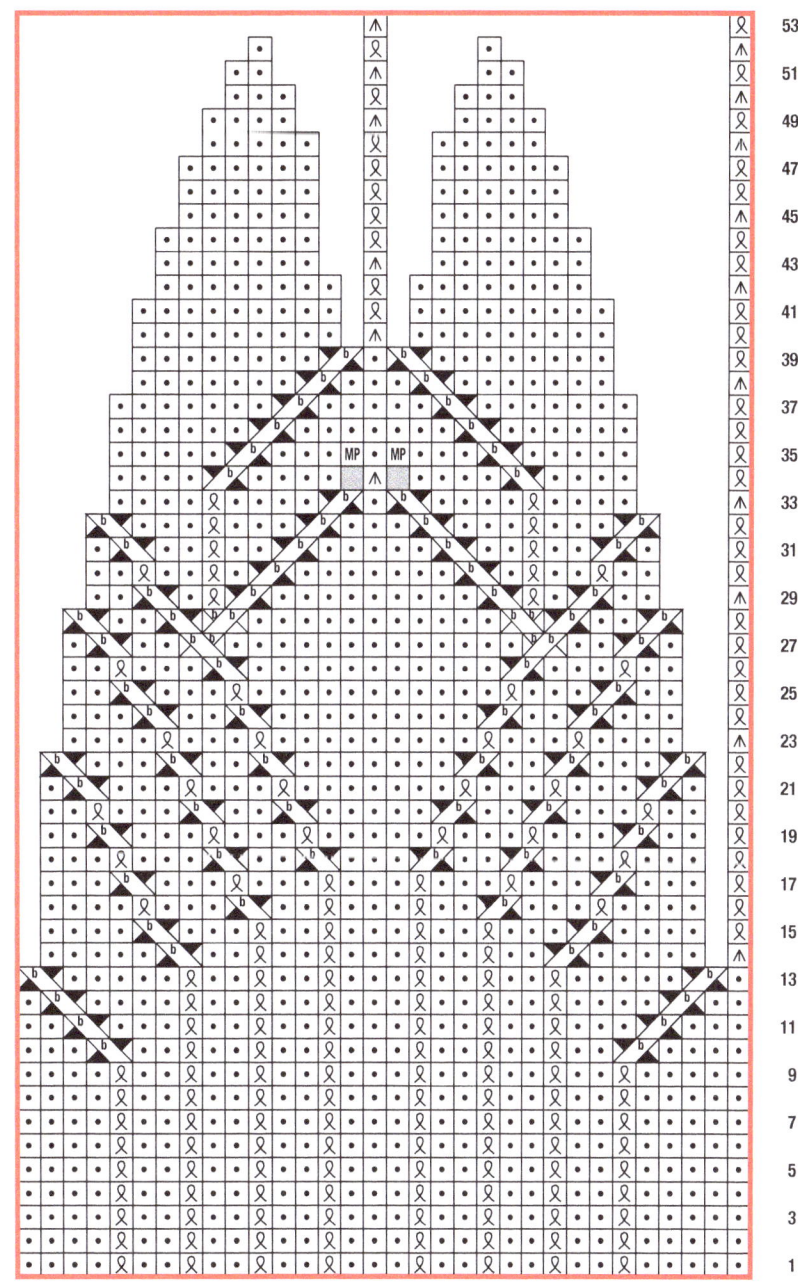

Skyscraper Hat

FARMERS' MARKET MITTS

Local culture often influences architecture, as seen in the textured knit/purl pattern on these fingerless mitts. It references the Pueblo influence seen in the architecture in Phoenix, Arizona, where I spent my high school years. Remembering how light and shadow play on adobe walls, these gently patterned mittens were born.

In milder climates where the mornings are cool but not freezing, these mitts make daybreak a bit cozier. Solid yarns work best for this project because the textured pattern is quite subtle.

Finished Size
7½ (8½, 9)" (19 [21.5, 23] cm) hand circumference and 5½ (6, 7¼)" (14 [15, 18.5] cm) long.

Mitts shown measure 8½" (21.5 cm).

Yarn
Fingering weight (#1 Super Fine).

Shown: Cascade Heritage Sock (75% superwash merino, 25% nylon; 437 yd [399.5 m]/100 g): #5681 Limestone, 1 skein.

Needles
Size U.S. 1 (2.25 mm): set of 4 or 5 double-pointed (dpn).

Size U.S. 2 (2.75 mm): set of 4 or 5 dpn.

U.S. size C-2 (2.75 mm) crochet hook.

Adjust needle and hook sizes if necessary to obtain the correct gauge.

Notions
Stitch markers (m); tapestry needle; waste yarn.

Gauge
33 sts and 54 rnds = 4" (10 cm) in chart patt with larger needles, blocked.

Knitting Knowledge
This project is worked in the round and requires:
- Knitting with circular and double-pointed needles
- Casting on
- Knitting and purling
- Reading charts
- Finishing

Note
The first row of this pattern is worked as a row so that it's easier to join the work for the first round without twisting the stitches.

CUFF

Cast on

With smaller dpn, CO 60 (68, 74) sts, using the German twisted method (Techniques, page 141).

NEXT ROW: [K1, p1] to end. Do not turn. Place marker (pm) for beg of rnd and join for working in rnds, being careful not to twist sts. Divide sts evenly over 3 or 4 dpn.

NEXT RND: [K1, p1] to end.

Rep last rnd until cuff measures 1" (2.5 cm) from CO.

INC RND: Work in established ribbing and inc 2 (2, 0) sts evenly—62 (70, 74) sts.

Change to larger dpn.

SET-UP RND: K1, pm, k30 (34, 36), pm, k1, pm, knit to end.

HAND

Begin chart

NEXT RND: *K1, sm, beg Rnd 1 of Chart A at arrow for your size and, reading sts from right to left, work 6 (5, 6) sts before rep, work 6-st rep 3 (4, 4) times, then work 6 (5, 6) sts after rep, sm; rep from * once more.

Work Rnds 2–24 of chart, then rep Rnds 1–24. *At the same time*, work thumb gusset when piece measures 2½ (2½, 3)" (6.5 [6.5, 7.5] cm) from CO.

THUMB GUSSET

INC RND 1: K1f/b/f, sm, work next chart row to m, slip marker (sm), k1, sm, work to end—64 (72, 76) sts; 61 (69, 73) sts for hand and 3 sts for gusset.

NEXT RND: Knit to m, sm, work in established patt to end.

INC RND 2: K1f&b, knit to 1 st before m, k1f&b, sm, work in established patt to end—2 sts inc'd for gusset.

Rep last 2 rnds 6 (7, 8) more times—78 (88, 94) sts; 61 (69, 73) sts for hand, and 17 (19, 21) sts for gusset.

NEXT RND: Remove beg-of-rnd marker, place next 16 (18, 20) sts onto waste yarn for thumb, replace beg-of-rnd marker, k1, work in established patt to end—62 (70, 74) sts rem.

PALM

NEXT RND: *K1, slip marker (sm), work next row of chart to next m, sm; rep from * once more.

Cont in established patt until piece measures 1 (1½, 2)" (2.5 [3.8, 5] cm) from held thumb sts or ¾" (2 cm) less than desired length, ending with Row 6 of the chart.

Change to smaller dpn.

NEXT RND: [K1, p1] to end.

Rep last rnd until ribbing measures ¾" (2 cm).

BO all sts loosely in patt. Cut yarn, leaving a 6" (15 cm) tail.

THUMB

Remove waste yarn and place held sts onto 3 dpn—16 (18, 20) sts.

Rejoin yarn to beg rnd at right edge of gusset.

NEXT RND: K16 (18, 20), pick up and k2 tbl in gap above thumb—18 (20, 22) sts.

Pm for beg of rnd and join to work in rnds. Divide sts evenly over 3 dpn.

Work in St st (knit every rnd) until thumb measures ¾ (¾, 1)" (2 [2, 2.5] cm) or desired thumb length.

BO all sts loosely. Cut yarn leaving a 6" (15 cm) tail.

FINISHING

Weave in all loose ends, waiting to cut yarn tails until after piece has been blocked. Make a second fingerless mitt exactly the same.

Soak finished mitts in cool water with a little wool wash. Lift out and gently squeeze to remove water. Lay mitts on a towel and roll up to remove excess water. Unroll, shape, and lay flat to dry.

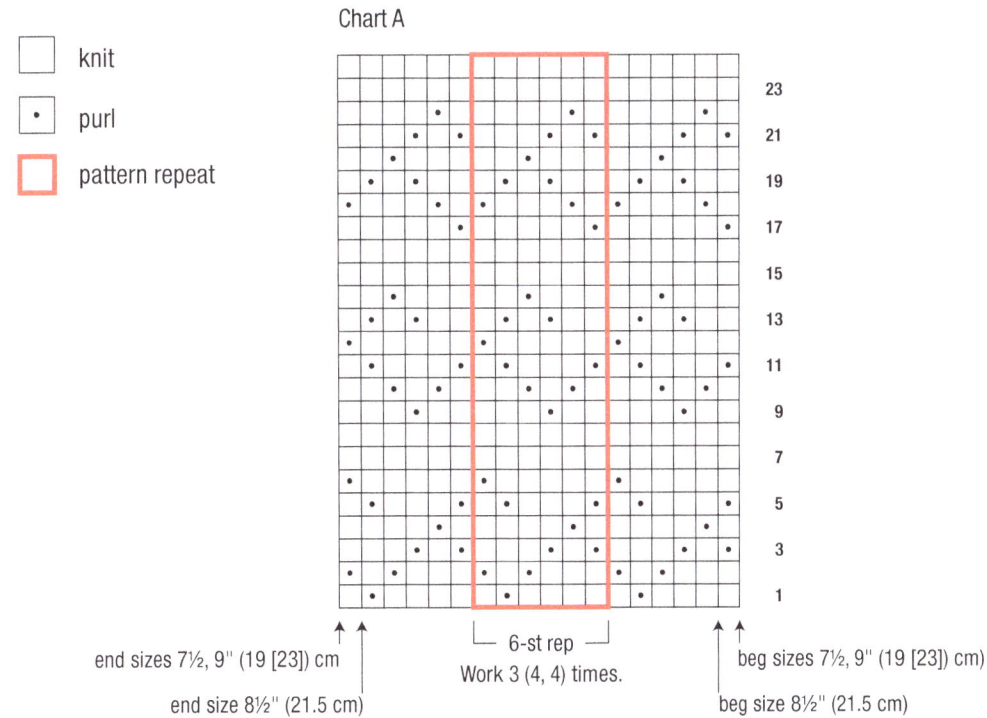

knit

• purl

pattern repeat

Chart A

23
21
19
17
15
13
11
9
7
5
3
1

end sizes 7½, 9" (19 [23]) cm
end size 8½" (21.5 cm)

6-st rep
Work 3 (4, 4) times.

beg sizes 7½, 9" (19 [23]) cm)
beg size 8½" (21.5 cm)

Farmers' Market Mitts

GLOSSARY

Abbreviations

beg:	begin(ning)
BO:	bind off
CC:	contrasting color
cir:	circular
CO:	cast on
cont:	continue(s); continuing
cn:	cable needle
dec('d):	decrease(s); decreasing; decreased
dpn:	double-pointed needle(s)
inc('d):	increase(s); increasing; increased
k:	knit
k1f&b:	knit into the front and back of the same stitch
k2tog:	knit two together
k2tog tbl:	knit two together through back loop
k1f/b/f:	knit into the front, back, then front of the same stitch
LH:	left hand
m:	marker(s)
m1:	make one (increase)
m1l:	make one (left slant)
m1p:	make 1 purlwise
m1r:	make one (right slant)
MC:	main color
p:	purl
patt(s):	pattern(s)
p2tog:	purl two together
pm:	place marker
psso:	pass slipped stitch(es) over
pwise:	purlwise, as if to purl
rem:	remain(ing)
rnd(s):	round(s)
RH:	right hand
RS:	right side
s2kp:	slip 2, k1, pass slipped stitches over
sl:	slip
sm:	slip marker
skp:	slip one, knit one, pass slipped stitch over
ssk:	slip, slip, knit (decrease)
ssp:	slip, slip, purl (decrease)
sk2p:	slip one stitch, knit 2 stitches together, pass slipped stitch over
st(s):	stitch(es)
St st:	stockinette stitch
tbl:	through back loop(s)
tog:	together
w&t:	wrap and turn
WS:	wrong side
wyb:	with yarn in back
wyf:	with yarn in front
yo:	yarn over

Techniques

CAST-ONS

Crochet Provisional Cast-On

Make a crochet chain 4 sts longer than the number of sts you need to cast on. Pick up and knit sts through back loops of crochet chain *(figure 1)*. Remove crochet chain to expose live stitches when you're ready to knit in opposite direction *(figure 2)*.

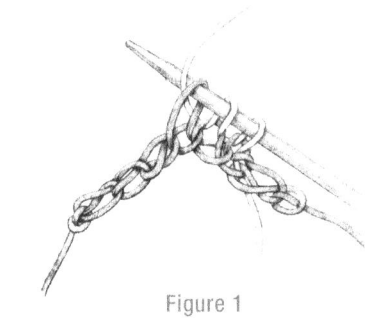

Figure 1

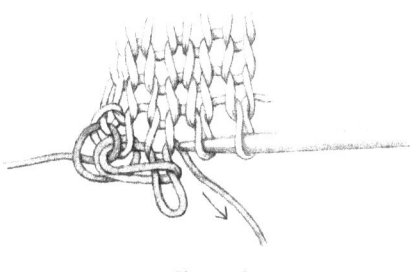

Figure 2

German Twisted Cast-On

Begin with a slipknot. Holding needle in your right hand, insert thumb and index finger between yarns *(figure 1)*. Move needle under yarn trailing off thumb *(figure 2)*, and then over the top and into loop *(figure 3)*. Move needle over loop, then under and around yarn on index finger. Move needle back through loop. Allow loop to slip off of thumb and pull gently to tighten.

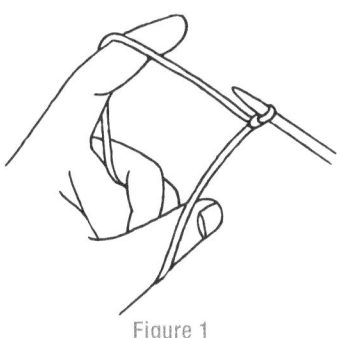

Figure 1

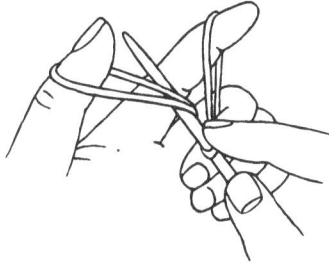

Figure 2

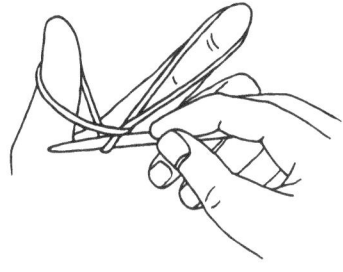

Figure 3

Glossary 141

BIND-OFFS

Standard Bind-Off

Knit first st, *knit next st (2 sts on RH needle), insert LH needle tip into first st on RH needle (*figure 1*) and lift st up and over second st (*figure 2*) and off needle (*figure 3*). Repeat from * for desired number of sts.

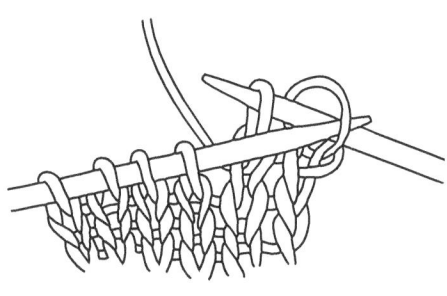

Figure 1

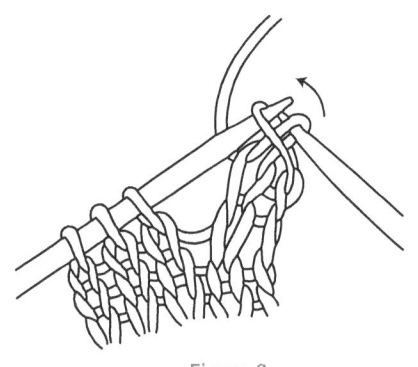

Figure 2

Figure 3

Decrease Bind-Off

*K2tog tbl (*figure 1*), slip st just worked back to LH needle tip (*figure 2*)—1 st decreased. Repeat from * to continue bind-off.

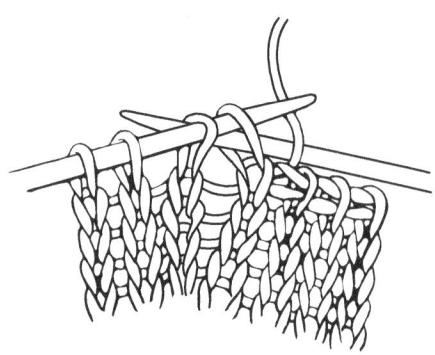

Figure 1

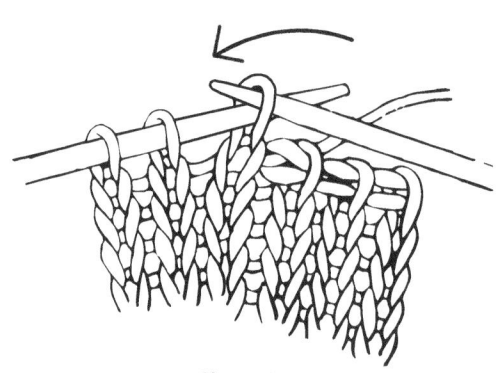

Figure 2

DECORATIVE STITCHES

Twisted Knit Stitch

RS: *K1 tbl, p1; repeat from *.
WS: Work sts as they appear.

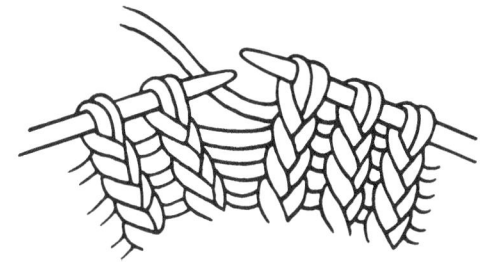

Duplicate Stitch

Horizontal: Bring threaded needle out from back to front at base of the V of the knitted stitch you want to cover. *Working right to left, pass needle in and out under st in the row above it and back into the base of the same st. Bring needle back out at base of the V of the next st to the left. Repeat from *.

Vertical: Beginning at lowest point, work as for horizontal duplicate stitch, ending by bringing needle back out at the base of st directly above the st just worked.

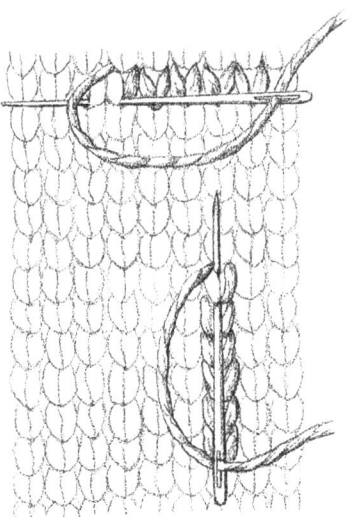

JOINING IN THE ROUND

Cast on number of stitches needed. Arrange cast-on sts so that "knots" are facing center of circle. Holding yarn in back, sl first st from LH needle to RH needle (*figure 1*), bring the yarn to front between needles, and sl first 2 sts from LH needle tip to RH needle tip (*figure 2*). Then bring yarn to back between needles and sl first st from RH needle tip back to LH needle tip (*figure 3*).

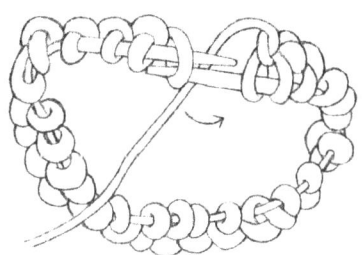

Figure 1

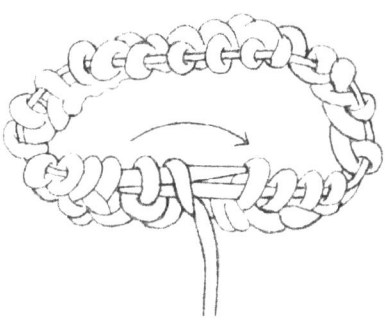

Figure 2

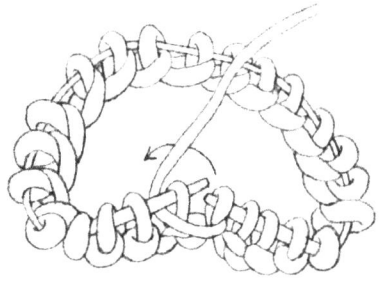

Figure 3

Glossary

RIBBING

K1, P1 Two-Color Ribbing

With RS facing, knit sts are worked in color A, and purl sts are worked in color B. When working RS rows, return both yarns to the back of the piece after working each stitch. When working WS rows, return both yarns to the front of the piece after working each stitch.

RS: *K1 with color A and leave yarn at back of work (*figure 1*). Move color B to front of work, p1, move color B to back of work (*figure 2*). Repeat from *.

WS: *P1 with color A and leave yarn at front of work. Move color B to back of work, k1, move color B to front of work. Repeat from *.

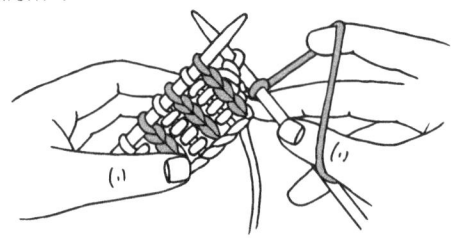

Figure 1

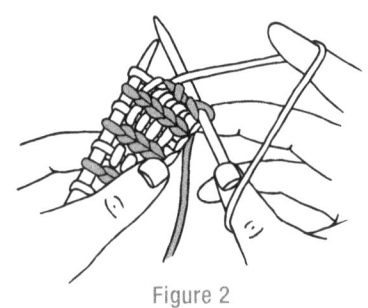

Figure 2

K1, P1 Ribbing

RS: *K1, p1; repeat from * to the end of the row (or to the last st, K1).

WS: *P1, k1; repeat from * to the end of the row (or to the last st, P1).

Repeat these 2 rows.

K2, P2 Ribbing

RS: *K2, p2; repeat from * to the end of the row) or to the last 2 sts, K2).

WS: *P2, k2; repeat from * to the end of the row (or to the last 2 sts, P2).

Repeat these 2 rows.

INCREASES

Make One—Right Slant (M1R)

With LH needle tip, lift strand between needles from back to front (*figure 1*). Knit lifted loop through the front (*figure 2*).

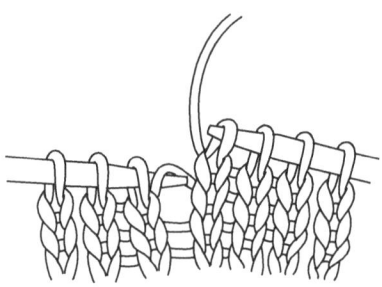

Figure 1

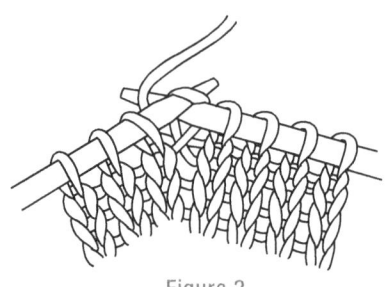

Figure 2

Make One—Left Slant (M1L)

With LH needle tip, lift strand between needles from front to back (*figure 1*). Knit lifted loop through the back (*figure 2*).

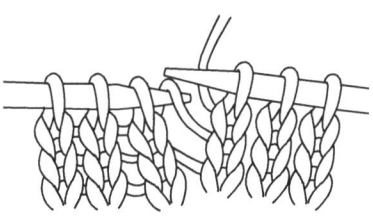

Figure 1

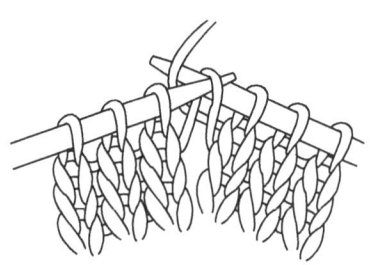

Figure 2

Knit into Front and Back (k1fb)

Knit into a stitch and leave it on LH needle (*figure 1*). Knit through back loop of the same stitch (*figure 2*). Sl sts off needle (*figure 3*).

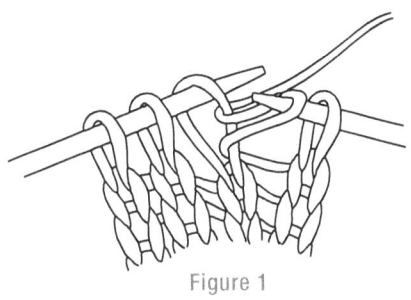

Figure 1

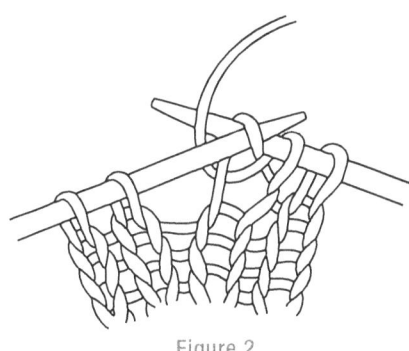

Figure 2

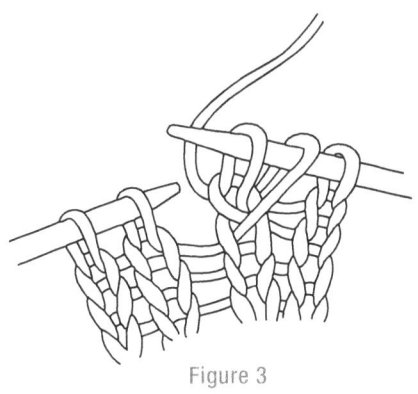

Figure 3

DECREASES

S2kp (sl 2, k1, psso)

Sl 2 sts as if to knit (*figure 1*), k1 (*figure 2*), pass both slipped sts over stitch just worked (*figure 3*) — 2 sts dec'd.

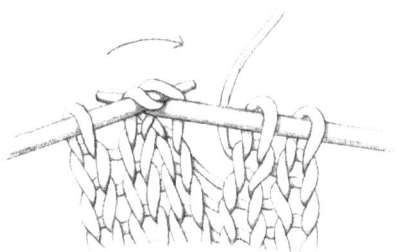

Figure 1

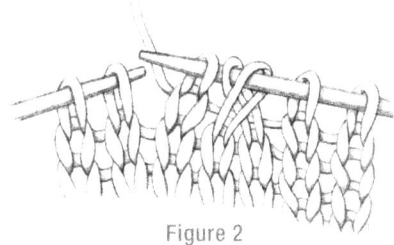

Figure 2

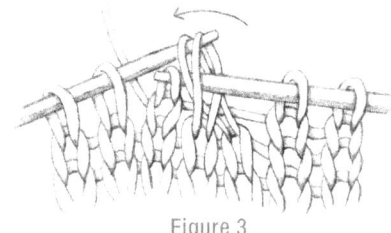

Figure 3

Sk2p (sl 1, k2, psso)

Slip first st as if to purl, knit next 2 sts together, pass first slipped st over the st just created (—2 sts dec'd).

Knit 2 Together (k2tog)

Knit 2 sts together as if they were a single stitch (*figure 1*).

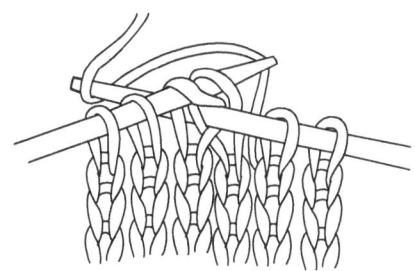

Figure 1

Glossary 145

Slip, Slip, Knit (ssk)

Sl 2 sts individually knitwise (*figure 1*), insert LH needle tip into front of 2 slipped sts, and use RH needle to knit them together through back loops (*figure 2*).

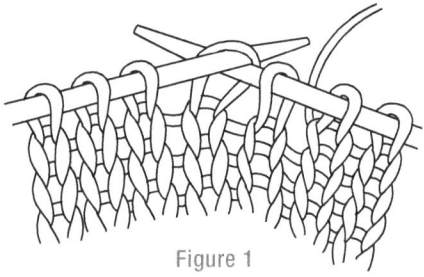
Figure 1

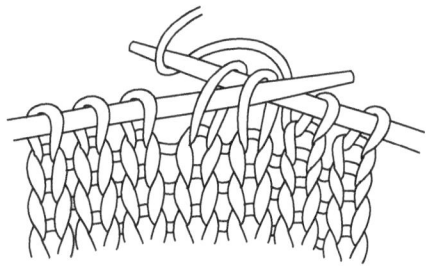
Figure 2

Slip, Slip, Purl (ssp)

Holding yarn in front, sl 2 sts individually knitwise (*figure 1*), then sl same 2 sts back onto LH needle (they will be turned on the needle) and purl them together through their back loops (*figure 2*).

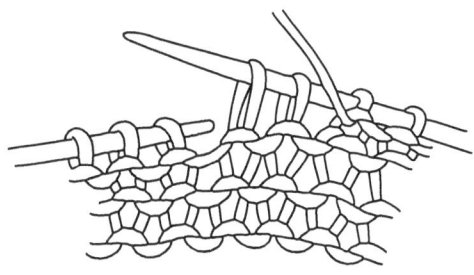
Figure 1

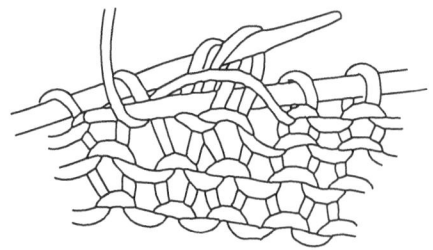
Figure 2

PICK UP AND KNIT

With RS facing and working from right to left, insert RH needle tip into center of stitch below the CO or BO edge (*figure 1*), wrap yarn around needle, and pull through a loop (*figure 2*). Pick up 1 st for every existing stitch.

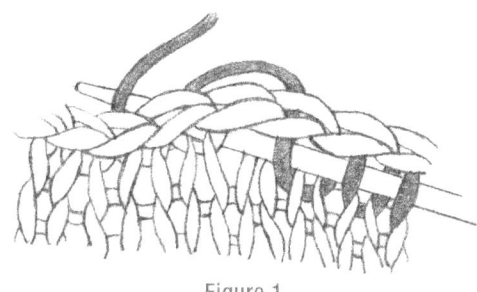
Figure 1

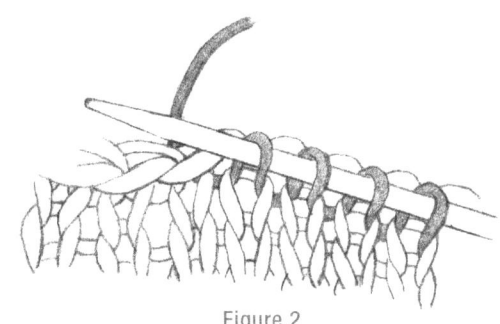
Figure 2

SHORT-ROWS

Wrap & Turn (w&t)

Knit row: With yarn in back, sl next st as if to purl *(figure 1)*, bring yarn to front. Sl st from RH needle back to LH needle *(figure 2)* and turn.

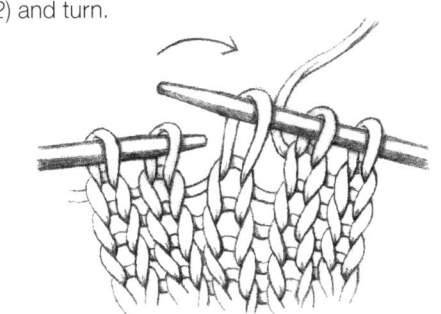

Figure 1

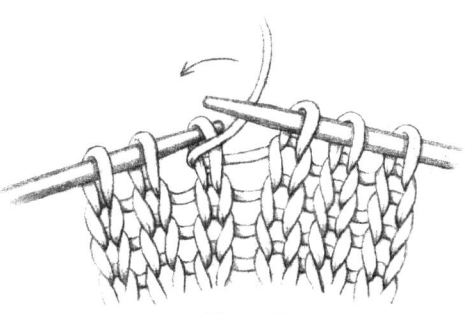

Figure 2

Purl row: With yarn in front, sl next st as if to purl, bring yarn to back *(figure 1)*. Sl st from the RH needle back to LH needle and Turn *(figure 2)*.

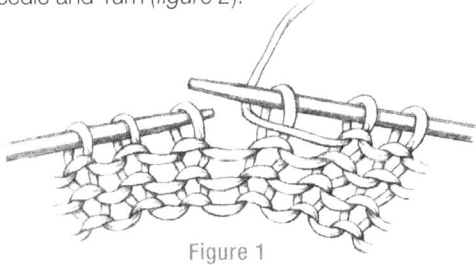

Figure 1

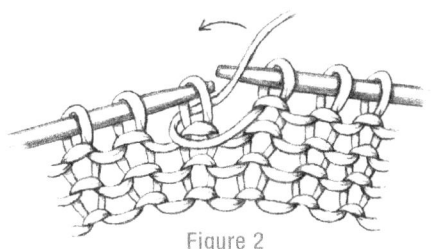

Figure 2

Hide Wrap

Knitting a wrapped stitch: Pick up wrap with RH needle from front to back *(figure 1)*. Insert RH needle into wrapped st. Knit together wrap and st.

Purling a wrapped stitch: Pick up wrap with RH needle from back to front. Place wrap onto LH needle *(figure 2)*. Purl together wrap and st.

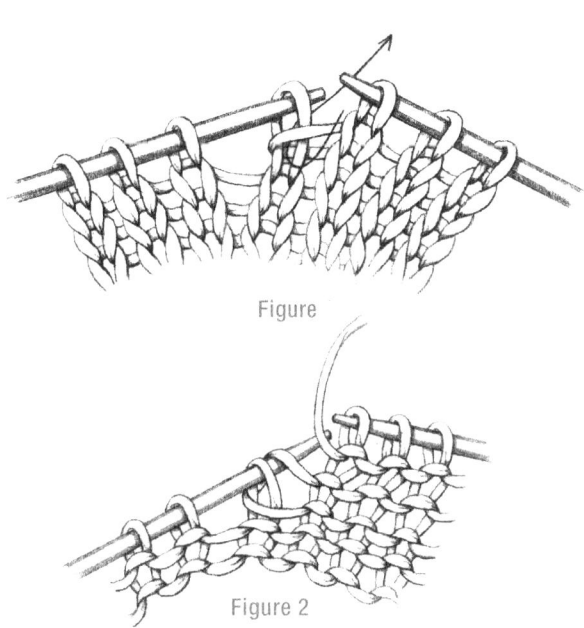

Figure

Figure 2

Glossary 147

GRAFTING

Kitchener Stitch

Arrange sts on two needles so there are the same number of sts on each needle. Hold needles parallel to each other with wrong sides of knitting together. Allowing about ½" (1.3 cm) per stitch to be grafted, thread matching yarn on tapestry needle. Work from right to left as follows:

Step 1

Bring tapestry needle through first st on front needle as if to purl and leave st on needle (*figure 1*).

Step 2

Bring tapestry needle through first st on back needle as if to knit and leave st on needle (*figure 2*).

Step 3

Bring tapestry needle through first front st as if to knit and sl st off needle, then bring tapestry needle through next front st as if to purl and leave st on needle (*figure 3*).

Step 4

Bring tapestry needle through first back st as if to purl and sl st off needle, then bring tapestry needle through next back st as if to knit and leave st on needle (*figure 4*).

Repeat Steps 3 and 4 until 1 st remains on each needle, adjusting tension to match the rest of the knitting as you go. To finish, bring tapestry needle through front st as if to knit and sl st off needle, then bring the tapestry needle through back st as if to purl and sl st off the needle.

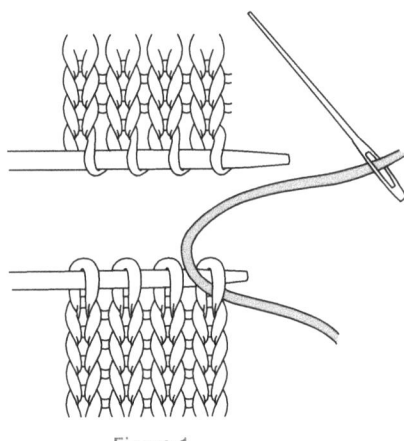

Figure 1

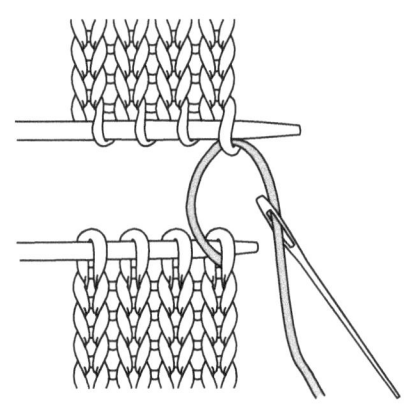

Figure 2

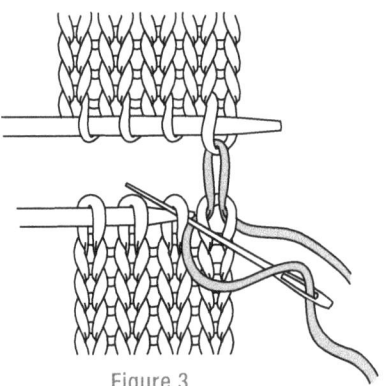

Figure 3

Figure 4

Invisible Vertical Seam (or Mattress Seam)

Place pieces to be seamed on a table, right sides facing up. Begin at lower edge and work upward as follows: Insert threaded needle under 1 bar between 2 edge sts on one piece *(figure 1)*, then under the corresponding bar plus the bar above it on the other piece *(figure 2)*. *Pick up next 2 bars on the first piece, then the next 2 bars on the other *(figure 3)*. Repeat from *, ending by picking up the last bar or pair of bars on the first piece.

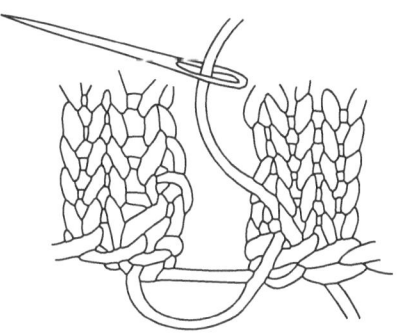

Figure 1

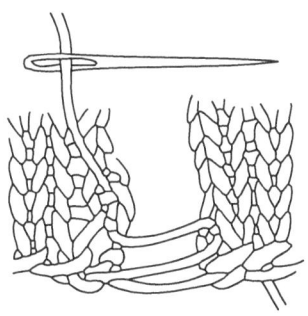

Figure 2

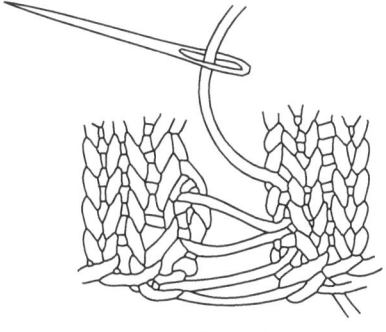

Figure 3

Vertical to Horizontal Grafting

*Bring threaded tapestry needle from back to front in the V of a knit stitch just below BO edge. Insert needle under 1 or 2 sts between the first and second st in from selvedge edge on adjacent piece, then back to front of same knit stitch just under BO edge *(figure 1)*. Repeat from *, taking care to match the tension of the knitting.

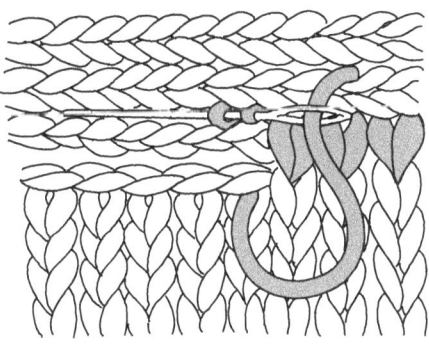

Figure 1

WEAVE IN LOOSE ENDS

Thread the yarn tail onto a tapestry needle and weave it in by following the path of a row of stitches (see figure 1), or work diagonally, catching the backs of the stitches (see figure 2). To avoid creating extra bulk, don't weave multiple ends into the same section.

If you're using a multi-plied yarn, you can separate the plies into two smaller strands and weave them in different directions for a smoother finish.

Always be sure to weave each end into stitches of the same color to help keep the back of your work looking tidy.

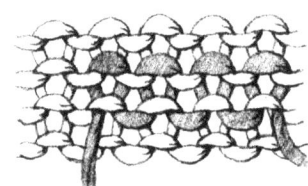

Figure 1

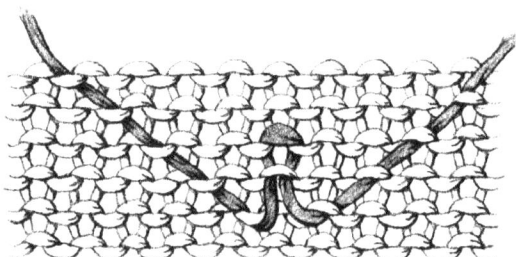

Figure 2

FELTED JOIN (AKA SPIT SPLICING)

A felted join works best on any 100 percent protein fiber, except silk. Some blends work well, too; the best way to know is to test it.

Remove about 2" (5 cm) of half the plies on each yarn tail to be joined. (If the yarn is a single, untwist and remove about half the mass.) Cross the tails at the center and fold the plies over each other to create a locked join (*figure 1*).

Add a bit of moisture to your palm (a drop of water, the condensation from a cold drink, or a little spit), and place the locked ends into your palm. Rub the yarn vigorously between your palms, generating heat, felting the plies together (*figure 2*).

Figure 1

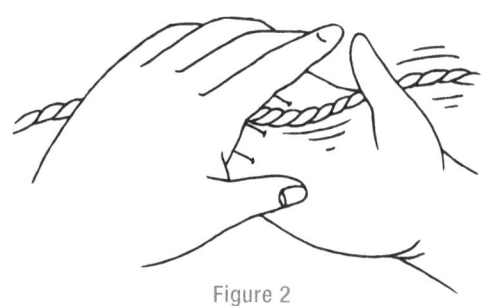

Figure 2

BUTTONHOLES

Work to where you want the buttonhole to begin, bring yarn to front, sl 1 st purlwise, bring yarn to back. *Sl 1 purlwise, pass first slipped st over second; repeat from * until desired number of sts have been bound off (figure 1). Place last st back on LH needle, turn.

Cast on above the opening as follows: *Insert RH needle between the first and second sts on LH needle, draw up a loop, and place it on the LH needle; repeat from * until desired number of sts have been cast on plus one more. Bring yarn to back, turn. Slip first st on left needle onto right needle and pass last cast-on st over it (figure 2), work to end of row.

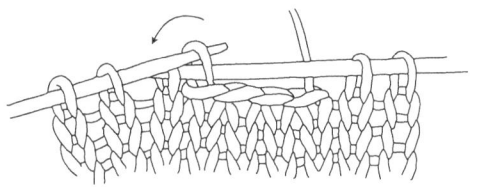

Figure 1

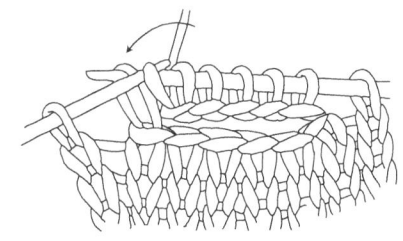

Figure 2

PLACE BEADS

For the "hooking-as-you-go" method, work to the next stitch that will receive a bead. Slide a bead onto a small crochet hook. Insert the hook into the next unworked stitch (figure 1), pull the yarn loop through the bead, and then place the loop back onto the left-hand (LH) needle (figure 2). Work the stitch as instructed to lock the bead in place.

Note: When when following the instructions above, the bead ultimately sits on the row or round below the one you're currently working. This is a natural result of placing the bead before working the stitch.

To place a bead so it appears on the current row or round (rather than the one below), first work the stitch as usual. Then, slip the completed stitch back onto the LH needle. Use the crochet hook to slide a bead onto the stitch, and finally return the beaded stitch to the right-hand (RH) needle. This method allows the bead to rest on top of the fabric, aligned with the current row or round.

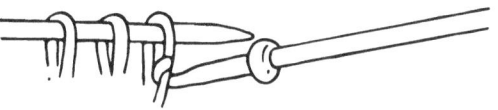

Figure 1

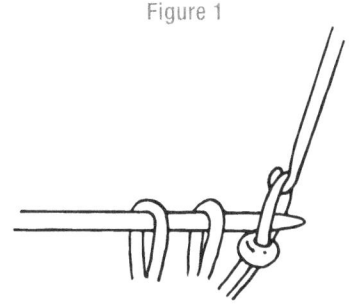

Figure 2

Glossary 151

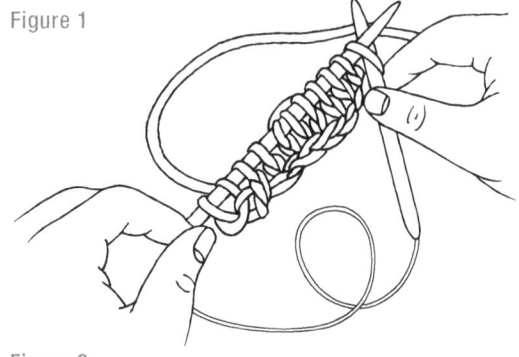

Figure 1

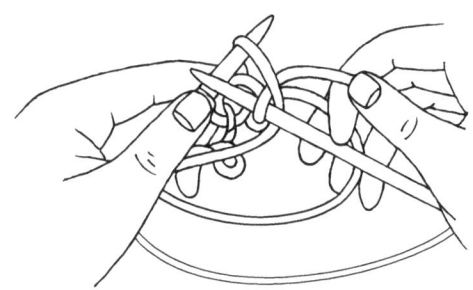

Figure 2

Figure 3

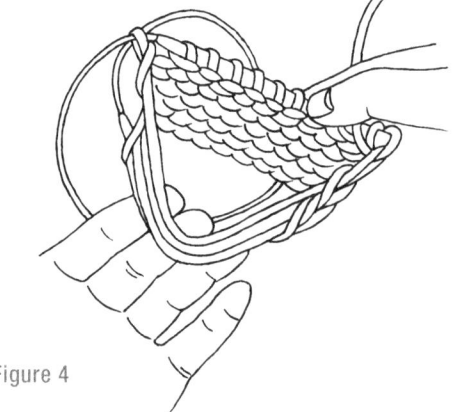

Figure 4

SPEED SWATCHING IN THE ROUND

With circular or double-pointed needles, work across a row, slide the work back to the right-hand needle (*figure 1*). Without turning, draw your yarn loosely across the back of the fabric to begin at the right side again (*figure 2*). Knit the first stitch or two carefully; they will be very loose (*figure 3*). The back of your work will have long strands of yarn from where you carried the yarn across for each row (*figure 4*).

Because you are knitting every row of the swatch, (instead of knitting a row, then purling a row), the gauge measurement will be more accurate. This method also saves you the time of casting on a larger number of stitches to join and swatch in the round.

When swatching for stranded projects, I use this time-saver: Gauge isn't determined by the stitch pattern, but by the needle size, yarn selection, and the number of yarns you're working *at the same time*. Regardless if you're working the colors in the order of the chart, you'll still end up with gauge!

When I'm knitting a gauge swatch for a stranded project, I cast on the number of stitches that will equal around 5" (12.5 cm). After a few rows of seed stitch in one color, I work a few stitches in seed stitch, and then join my second color. I knit a few stitches in color A, then a few in color B, alternating between the two colors in a random order until the last few stitches of the row. I finish in seed stitch using the main color.

When working a flat swatch, I continue this random coloring method, purling the stitches in the same color order as in the previous row. From here on, right-side rows are knit in whatever color order I want, and wrong-side rows are worked following the color order of the previous row. The pattern resembles zebra print. Once I have a swatch big enough to measure a 5" (12.5 cm) square, I complete it with another seed-stitch border using the main color. If I like what I see, then a wash and block will tell me for sure that my needle and yarn combo yields the stitch and row count I want for my project.

SHAPING IN COLORWORK

Shaping—increasing or decreasing—in colorwork should be done in pattern. For example, when working an SSK, look at the two stitches you're about to combine (*figure 1*) and perform the decrease with the color indicated by the chart over the leftmost stitch (*figure 2*). This decrease leans to the left and eliminates the leftmost stitch.

Even if the two stitches being combined aren't the same color, the rule still applies. Look at the two stitches about to be combined (*figure 3*) and work the decrease in the same color as the leftmost stitch (*figure 4*).

When working a K2tog, look at the two stitches you're about to combine. Perform this decrease with the color indicated by the chart over the rightmost stitch. This decrease leans to the right and eliminates the rightmost stitch.

When working flat, I usually work decreases and increases two stitches in from the edge and stick to whatever decrease type I selected throughout the project. This keeps the location of the shaping the same on each row and helps make a nice finish. Often, I'll also keep the two edge stitches in the same color so that when the work is seamed up, there's a small border highlighting the seam.

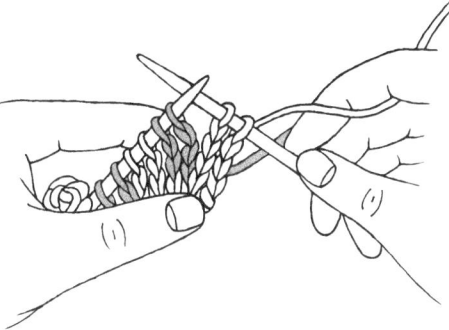

Figure 1

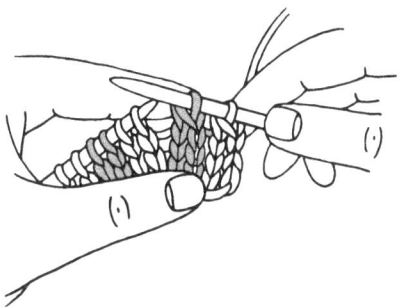

Figure 2

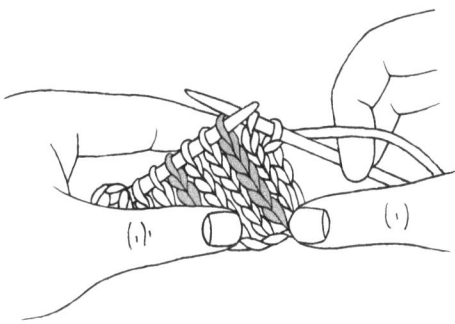

Figure 3

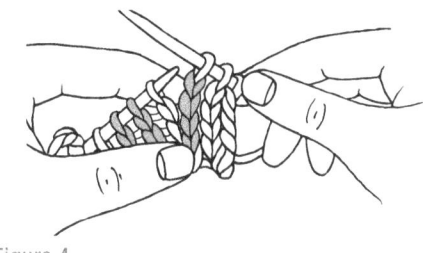

Figure 4

SHORT-ROWS IN COLORWORK

Short-rows shape fabric by allowing you to stop partway through a row or round, turn your work, and continue in the opposite direction (Techniques, page 141). One common method involves wrapping the yarn around the next stitch before turning, which helps minimize gaps when you later return to work across those stitches. There are several ways to work short-rows—some more visible than others—and while many are interchangeable, some patterns may rely on the specific structure of a wrap-and-turn or another method. When in doubt, swatch.

In stranded colorwork, wrap the stitch using the same color as the one you're working with. Later, when picking up the wraps, the wrapped stitch and its wrap will blend into the surrounding fabric. As you progress, you'll notice that wrapped sections won't always line up neatly with your chart—that's normal. When you finally work across those wraps, follow the established color pattern. In areas like shoulders, where short-rows are often used, the shaping typically falls near a seam, and any visual disruption is minimal.

If you'd like to add structure or detail, you can intentionally highlight these areas. Try picking up all wraps with the same color and binding off in that color to create a faux seam. When mirrored and seamed on two matching pieces, it forms a clean visual edge.

Still deciding which short-row method to use? Experiment on your swatch. It's far less painful to rip out ten rows of a practice piece than ten rows on the actual sweater (ask me how I know).

MEASURING GAUGE

Knit a swatch that measures at least 5" (12.5 cm) square. Once complete, either bind off loosely or remove the stitches from the needles. Lay the swatch flat on a smooth surface and use a ruler to measure a 4" (10 cm) section. Count the number of stitches across and rows (or rounds) down within that section—include any partial stitches or rows. Divide these counts by 4 to determine the number of stitches and rows per inch (2.5 cm). Measure in a few different areas of the swatch to confirm consistency.

If you have more stitches or rows than the pattern calls for, try swatching again with larger needles. If you have fewer, switch to smaller needles.

Always swatch using the same type of needles—wood, metal, etc.—that you plan to use for the actual project, as different materials can affect your gauge.

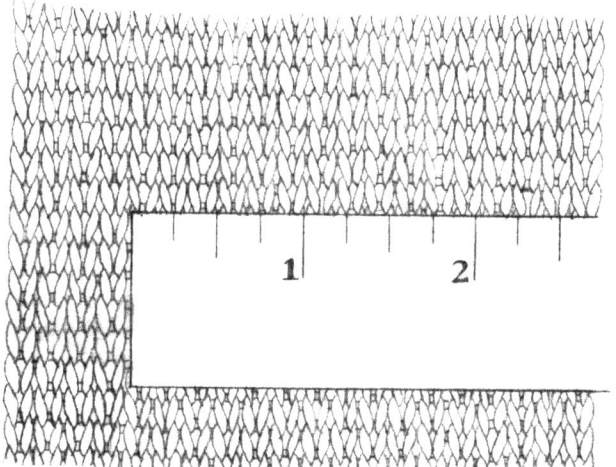

BIBLIOGRAPHY

Arwas, Victor. *Art Deco.* New York: Abrams, 1980.

Bayer, Patricia. *Art Deco Interiors: Decoration and Design Classics of the 1920s and 1930s.* London: Thames & Hudson, 1999.

Breeze, Carla. *American Art Deco: Architecture and Regionalism.* New York: W. W. Norton, 2003.

Capitman, Barbara Baer, Michael D. Kinerk, Dennis W. Wilhelm, and Randy Juster. *Rediscovering Art Deco U.S.A.* New York: Viking Studio, 1994.

Crowe, Michael F. *Deco by the Bay: Art Deco Architecture in the San Francisco Bay Area.* New York: Viking Studio, 1995.

Duncan, Alastair. *American Art Deco.* New York: Abrams, 1986.

——— *Art Deco.* London: Thames and Hudson, 1988.

——— *The Encyclopedia of Art Deco.* New York: E. P. Dutton, 1988.

Gallagher, Fiona, Michael Jeffery, Simon Andrews, and Nicolette White. Christie's Art Deco. New York: Watson-Guptill, 2000.

Gebhard, David. *The National Trust Guide to Art Deco in America.* New York: J. Wiley, 1996.

Hillier, Bevis. *The World of Art Deco.* New York: E. P. Dutton, 1971.

Klein, Dan. *All Color Book of Art Deco.* London: Octopus, 1974.

Schwartzman, Arnold. *Deco Landmarks: Art Deco Gems of Los Angeles.* San Francisco: Chronicle Books, 2005.

Sease, Catherine. *Cast On, Bind Off: 211 Ways to Begin and End Your Knitting.* Bothell: Martingale, 2012.

Weber, Eva. *American Art Deco.* North Dighton: JG/World Publications Group, 2004.

INDEX

beads, adding 95
bind-offs 92, 142
buttonholes 151

cast-ons 92, 141
charts, tips for reading large 81
colorwork shaping 153
colorwork short-rows 154
crochet provisional cast-on 141

decorative stitches 143
decrease bind-off 74, 142
decreases 145–146
duplicate stitch 143

ends, weaving in 150

floats, locking 11–15

gauge 154
German twisted cast-on 141
grafting 148; vertical to horizontal 149

hide wrap 147

I-cord, applied 120
increases 144–145
join, felted 150
joining in the round 143

Kitchener stitch 148
knit into front and back (k1fb) 145
knit 2 together (k2tog) 145

make one (M1) 144
mattress stitch 149
mistakes, fixing 10

pick up and knit 146
provisional cast-ons 141

ribbing 144
ripping out 10

seam, invisible vertical 149; mattress 149
seed stitch bind-off 92
short-rows 154
skill level 9
slip, slip, knit (ssk) 146
slip, slip, purl (ssp) 146
speed swatching in the round 152
spit splicing 150
stranded-knitting swatch 9
standard bind-off 142
sk2p (sl 1, k2, psso) 145
s2kp (sl 2, k1, psso) 145
swatching 9, 152

twisted knit stitch 143

vertical to horizontal grafting 149

wrap & turn (w&t) 147

yarn splicing 150
yarns, bleeding 9

THE JOURNEY CONTINUES

The wrap shown here is Cutrera—a bold, large-scale design that uses locked floats and multiple charts to create a stunning finished project. It's the kind of piece that asks you to slow down, stay focused, and trust the process.

Remember: knitting isn't difficult, it just takes time.
One stitch after another, you can make anything you want!

Thank you for spending part of your creative time with me. Whether you're refining familiar skills or learning something new, I hope these pages have sparked ideas, built confidence, and encouraged you to explore knitting in your own way.

Scan the QR code to visit my website:
kylewilliam.com

ACKNOWLEDGMENTS

Publishing this revised second edition has given me the opportunity to revisit a project that still means so much to me. While the patterns remain unchanged, this update is a chance to reflect on the people and experiences that helped shape the original collection—and the continued encouragement I've received along the way.

To **my family**: thank you for your love, patience, and steady support. I'm especially grateful to my mother and grandmothers, whose creativity and care sparked my passion for making. Your influence runs through every stitch.

To **John Silowsky** and **Chuck Blank**—thank you for your unwavering support and for graciously living among mountains of yarn and endless swatches.

To **Chuck Wilmesher**—your encouragement at every turn still means the world. And to **Keith Leonard**, your humor, honesty, and friendship—paired with Chuck's—have lifted me more than you know.

To **Kate Godfrey**—your early guidance helped shape this book into something real, and every time I sit down to write, I still hear your voice reminding me: "One space after a period." Thank you for that, and so much more.

To **Cynthia Baily, Aaron Bush, Andrea Brooks,** and **Jody Strine**—your talent and generosity brought these designs to life. I remain deeply grateful for the role each of you played in the original collection.

To **Karin Skacel**—your unwavering support has changed my life in more ways than I can count. Your generosity, belief in my work, and constant encouragement have helped me grow not only as a designer, but as a person. You are more than a mentor or friend—you're family. Thank you for always being in my corner.

To **Kerry Bogert**—thank you for being the first person to say "yes" to this book. Your guidance through the original proposal process—and the months of thoughtful revision that followed—helped shape its foundation. Your support didn't end there; your insight and care during the development of this second edition have been equally invaluable. You remain a steady source of encouragement and empowerment, and I'm so grateful for our friendship!

To **Louisa Demmitt**—thank you for being the kind of collaborator and friend every creative person hopes to have. Whether we're tackling projects or laughing at something completely ridiculous, your insight, humor, and steady encouragement have made this book—and life—better in every way. Your support has been as delightful as pickles on a grilled cheese—now that I know life with it, I can't imagine it any other way.

To **Marie Greene**—you are a true friend, a source of steady strength, and one of the brightest lights in my creative life. You lift others up, lead with heart, and empower those around you to do bold, beautiful things. I'm grateful for your wisdom, your laughter, and your unwavering belief in me.

To **Hayes Russock**—thank you for showing up with steady presence, quiet strength, and the kind of friendship that makes even the most ordinary days feel less heavy. Even when there's not much to say, our conversations remind me I'm not alone. I'm deepful grateful for your loyalty, your listening ear, and the comfort of knowing you're always there.

To **BeLinda Creech**—thank you for your friendship, your brilliant ideas, and the spark you bring to our daily conversations. I'm so proud of you for getting your college degree, and for how fully you show up for the people around you. Your off-the-wall brainstorming ideas have a magical way of turning into something truly great - and the world is brighter (and possibly more at risk of receiving a random potato in the mail) because of you!

And finally, to **you**—thank for spending time with these pages, for exploring this work, and for the creative energy you bring to your own hobbies. Whether it's charting colorwork, frogging a sleeve, or casting on just because it felt right—or simply being here to learn someting new—your presence is part of what makes this community so vibrant.

Not every project needs to be finished. What matters is that we enjoy the process of making, with or without weaving in all the ends!

—Kyle Kunnecke

A DAVID AND CHARLES BOOK
© Kyle Kunnecke 2025

David and Charles is an imprint of David and Charles, Ltd
Suite A, Tourism House, Pynes Hill, Exeter, EX2 5WS

First published in the UK and USA in 2016 by Interweave
This edition first published in 2025 by David and Charles

Kyle Kunnecke has asserted his right to be identified as author of this work in accordance with the Copyright, Designs and Patents Act, 1988.

All rights reserved. No part of this publication may be reproduced in any form or by any means, electronic or mechanical, by photocopying, recording or otherwise, without prior permission in writing from the publisher.

No part of this publication may be used or reproduced in any manner for the purpose of training artificial intelligence technologies or systems without permission from David and Charles Ltd.

Readers are permitted to reproduce any of the designs in this book for their personal use and without the prior permission of the publisher. However, the designs in this book are copyright and must not be reproduced for resale.

The author and publisher have made every effort to ensure that all the instructions in the book are accurate and safe, and therefore cannot accept liability for any resulting injury, damage or loss to persons or property, however it may arise.

Names of manufacturers and product ranges are provided for the information of readers, with no intention to infringe copyright or trademarks.

A catalogue record for this book is available from the British Library.

ISBN-13: 9781446318065 paperback

Editor: Leslie T. O'Neill
Technical Editor: Therese Chynoweth
Cover Design: Kerry Bogert
Interior Design: Amy Petriello
Photographer: Donald Scott
Photo Stylist: Tina Gill
Hair & Makeup: Kathy MacKay

David and Charles publishes high-quality books on a wide range of subjects. For more information visit www.davidandcharles.com

Share your makes with us on social media using #dandcbooks and follow us on Facebook and Instagram by searching for @dandcbooks.

www.ingramcontent.com/pod-product-compliance
Lightning Source LLC
Chambersburg PA
CBHW061811230426

43665CB00033BA/2999